AWESOME EXPERIMENTS IN

Electricity
&
Magnetism

WITHDRAWN

Michael A. DiSpezio

Illustrated by Rob Collinet

Sterling Publishing Co., Inc.
New York

Library of Congress Cataloging-in-Publication Data Available

10 9 8 7 6 5 4 3 2 1

Published by Sterling Publishing Co., Inc.
387 Park Avenue South, New York, NY 10016
© 2006 by Sterling Publishing Co., Inc.
Illustrations © 2006 by Rob Collinet
Previously published © 1998 by Michael A. DiSpezio
Distributed in Canada by Sterling Publishing
c/o Canadian Manda Group, 165 Dufferin Street,
Toronto, Ontario, Canada M6K 3H6
Distributed in the United Kingdom by GMC Distribution Services,
Castle Place, 166 High Street, Lewes, East Sussex, England BN7 1XU
Distributed in Australia by Capricorn Link (Australia) Pty. Ltd.
P.O. Box 704, Windsor, NSW 2756, Australia

Sterling ISBN-13: 978-1-4027-2370-4
          ISBN-10: 1-4027-2370-9

For information about custom editions, special sales, premium and cor-
porate purchases, please contact Sterling Special Sales
Department at 800-805-5489 or specialsales@sterlingpub.com.

Contents

PART TWO
Current Electricity

PART ONE

Static
Electricity

All Charged Up

Most of us imagine electricity as a flow of energy along wires that lights bulbs, spins motors, and rings bells. This type of moving energy is called *current electricity.* But there's another type of electricity that behaves differently from this flowing form. It's called *static electricity.*

The dictionary defines the word "static" as stationary or non-moving. In other words, when something is static, it stays put. This first experiment will introduce you to this fun and fundamental form of electricity.

Materials
- ❏ two balloons
- ❏ a piece of wool or felt
- ❏ adhesive tape
- ❏ a piece of thread 1 foot (30 cm) long

To Do

Inflate two balloons. Attach a 1-foot (30 cm) length of thread to each of the balloons. Use tape to attach the thread of one balloon to the bottom of a desk (or the roof of a favorite hideout).

Rub the hanging balloon with a piece of wool or felt. You should give it at least twenty back-and-forth rubs. Release this balloon and let it hang.

Rub the second balloon with the wool or felt. Hold it by the end of the thread and bring it near the first balloon. What happens to the balloons? Tape the second balloon close enough to the first so that they appear to be flying away from each other.

The Science

Most objects start off with a neutral charge. Rubbing them with certain materials can cause an exchange of minute, invisible particles called electrons that can change that.

As you rubbed a balloon with the wool, invisible negatively charged particles flowed from the wool onto the balloon. As a result, the balloon's charge balance was changed. The added charge gave the balloon a net negative charge. Once transferred, the tiny charges stayed put (hence the "static" in static electricity).

At a distance, the two charged balloons did not have enough charge to affect each other. When they got closer, however, things changed. Since both balloons had a negative charge, they repelled each other. This force caused them to move away from each other and remain apart.

Check It Out! Suppose a third charged balloon was brought near these two. What shape would the repelling balloons form?

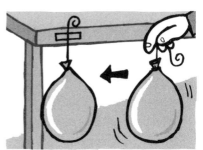

In the previous experiment, we created a negative charge on a balloon when we rubbed it with wool. Because the balloon now has more negative charges than positive charges, it has a net negative charge. This type of "charging" is called *contact charging.*

Contact charging can also produce objects with a positive charge. For an object's charge to become positive, it must lose some of its negative charges. This loss offsets the neutral balance to produce a net positive charge.

Materials

❑ 10-inch (25 cm) strip of nylon fabric (if needed, cut the nylon from a stocking)
❑ a pair of scissors
❑ a plastic grocery bag

To Do

Use your scissors to cut a 10-inch (25 cm) strip of nylon. Firmly hold the middle of the strip, allowing the halves to hang downward. Grasp the nylon with the plastic bag. Stroke both halves of the fabric several times. What happens when you stop stroking the nylon? What causes the nylon to behave this way?

The Science

Unlike wool, plastic does not easily give up its negative electrons. On the contrary, it has a tendency to take in negative electrons. When the plastic rubbed against the nylon, negative charges transferred from the fabric to the plastic material. This left the nylon strips with a positive charge. Since both hanging halves had the same charge, they repelled each other, causing the free ends to separate.

Check It Out! Can you charge a plastic bag by rubbing it with wool?

1.3 Main Attraction

So far, you've observed what happens when objects of the same charge are brought together. The negatively charged balloons repel each other. The positively charged nylon strips repel each other. But what happens when a negative balloon and a positive nylon strip are brought near each other?

Materials

- ❑ nylon strip
- ❑ 1-foot (30 cm) length of thread
- ❑ adhesive tape
- ❑ a balloon
- ❑ a plastic grocery bag

To Do

Attach a 1-foot (30 cm) length of thread to an inflated balloon. Charge the balloon by rubbing it with wool. Use tape to attach the thread to the edge of a table or desk.

Charge the nylon strip by rubbing it with a plastic bag. Stroke the strip several times to ensure that it becomes sufficiently charged. Bring the strip near the hanging balloon. What happens?

Release the strip. Does it stick to the balloon or is it repelled by this oppositely charged object?

The Science

Like charges repel. Unlike charges attract.

Both the balloon and strip were charged by contact

charging. The balloon took on a net negative charge. The nylon strip took on a net positive charge.

When the negative and positive charges were close enough, the objects moved together. At close range, the attraction was strong enough to stick the nylon to the balloon's surface.

Check It Out! Can rubbing with nylon or a paper towel produce contact charging?

Static Glue

Birthday parties occur throughout the year. Most likely, you've attended parties that had balloon decorations. Did you ever notice that by rubbing the balloons and placing them against the wall, they would magically cling to the dry flat surface. Why?

Materials

- ❑ a balloon
- ❑ a piece of wool or felt

To Do

Inflate a balloon and stroke it with a piece of wool or felt. If you don't have any fabric, you can stroke the balloon against your hair. Place the balloon against the wall. What happens? How long will the balloon cling to the wall? Recharge the balloon and observe how well it clings to other objects, such as wood, a metal cabinet, and glass.

The Science

As the balloon is rubbed with wool, it becomes negatively charged. This charge produces an invisible electric field.

When the balloon is brought close to the wall, the negative charges in the wall are repelled by the approaching negative field. These charges respond by moving away from the nearing balloon. This leaves the region closest to the wall surface with a relative positive charge. As a result, the positive wall surface and the negative balloon attract, causing the balloon to stick to the upright surface.

The wall became charged by *induction*. In this type of charging, objects don't touch. Instead an electric field causes charges to migrate in surrounding materials. Although the number of charges remains the same, they are unequally distributed. Regions with more positive charges take on a net positive charge. Regions with more negative charges take on a net negative charge.

Check It Out! Can you charge up a balloon if you alternate the direction of the strokes?

Charge It On Plastic

Have you ever sat on a plastic lawn chair and placed your bare arms on the chair's surface? If so, you may have felt a "clinging" force sticking to your tiny arm hairs. This force is produced by the charged plastic. As your body shifted in the chair, electrons were transferred to the plastic material to produce a "sticky" sensation.

Materials

❑ two strips of plastic (cut from an overhead transparency or report cover)
❑ paper
❑ a pair of scissors

To Do

Use the scissors to cut two separate strips of plastic, each about 2 inches (5 cm) wide x 10 inches (25 cm) long. Place the strips side by side on a sheet of plain white paper.

Hold a strip down with your fingers and stroke it about ten times. Do this to both strips.

Pick up the strips by their edges and hold them together so that they hang freely. What do you notice about the plastic strips? Do they hang freely or is there an invisible force at work?

The Science

As your fingers rubbed against the plastic, electrons were transferred. This produced an electric charge in the plastic. Since both hanging strips had the same charge, they repelled each other and hung apart.

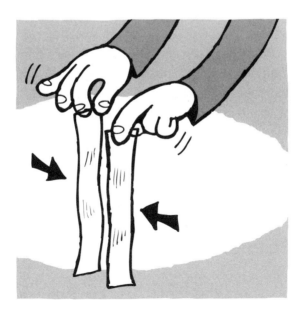

1.6 Ghost Legs

The magician covers a box with a silk scarf. Slowly she raises the box into the air. While holding the covered box, she suddenly flicks her wrist. The scarf goes limp and the box disappears. How did she do it? We're not telling, but we do have a magical activity that also produces a phantom shape in thin air.

Materials

❑ a sheer nylon stocking
❑ a plastic grocery bag
❑ a smooth wall

To Do

With one hand, hold the top of the stocking flat against a wall. Use the other hand to stroke the stocking in one direction with the plastic grocery bag. As you stroke the nylon material, smooth it against the wall's surface.

After several strokes, release the stocking. What happens to the material? How is this similar to sticking balloons to a wall? How is it different?

Now gently grasp the top of the stocking and move it away from the wall. Make sure that it does not touch anything (including yourself). Hold out the stocking. What happens to its shape? Can you explain your observation?

The Science

As the plastic bag moves over the nylon, it picks up negative charges. This produces a stocking with a net positive charge. This charged stocking acts like the negatively charged balloon and induces an opposite charge in the nearby wall. The negative and positive charges attract and the stocking clings to the wall. When the stocking is moved away from the wall, it still retains its net positive charge. These charges, which are distributed throughout the stocking material, push away from each other. This causes the stocking to "expand" and take on the leg shape in which it was manufactured.

1.7 Push and Pull

Objects that have like charges repel.

Objects that have unlike charges attract.

But what happens when one object has a charge and the other one is neutral? Can you guess how these objects will react, based on what you have observed in the previous experiments?

Materials

- ❑ two balloons
- ❑ two 1-foot-long (30 cm) threads
- ❑ adhesive tape
- ❑ a piece of wool

To Do

Inflate two balloons. Tie a 1-foot (30 cm) section of thread to each. Position the balloons so that they hang side by side, separated by several inches of space. Hold one of the balloons and stroke it with wool. Once this balloon has been charged, gently let it fall back into place. As it moves into its original position, what happens to the nearby neutral balloon? Can you explain what caused this action?

The Science

The balloon that was stroked with wool picked up a net negative charge. This charge initially repelled the negative charges in the neighboring balloon. As those negative charges moved to other regions of the balloon material, the nearby area became positive in charge. Attraction between the negative balloon and positive region of the neighboring balloon drew these charged objects together.

1.8 Charge the Comb

On a dry, crisp day, find a totally quiet room. Comb your hair and listen carefully. Do you hear anything?

Materials
- ❑ a plastic comb
- ❑ paper

To Do
Tear up a sheet of paper into small pieces. Place these pieces in a small pile on a table.

Run a plastic comb through your hair several times. Then position the comb above the pile of paper. What happens?

The Science
Paper, like most materials, starts out with an equal and random distribution of negative and positive charges. Since the charges are equal in number, they cancel each other out so that the paper has a net neutral charge.

As the comb rubs against hair, negative charges are transferred onto the comb. Through contact, the comb takes on a net negative charge.

When the comb is placed above the paper, it exerts its negative field, which causes the negative charges in the paper to move away from the comb. These negative charges migrate through the paper and collect at the paper's far side. Through *induction,* the closer region becomes positive.

The attraction between this positive region of the paper and the negative comb is strong enough to overcome gravity. The paper pieces jump from the tabletop to the comb.

As the paper clings to the comb, the comb's negative charges migrate into the paper. This cancels the nearby charge and the paper falls to the tabletop.

Check It Out! Would pieces of aluminum foil or plastic wrap behave like the paper?

1.9 Barrel Roll

So far, you've learned that paper sticks well to combs. But did you know you can move a rolled-up piece of paper by static attraction? Here's how.

Materials

- ❑ paper
- ❑ a pair of scissors
- ❑ adhesive tape
- ❑ a plastic comb
- ❑ wool

To Do

Cut out a strip of paper about 1 inch (2.5 cm) wide and 4 inches (10 cm) long. Roll the paper into a bracelet-like shape and secure its shape with a small section of tape. Stand the "barrel" on its side. Charge up the comb by running it through your hair or stroking it with a piece of wool or flannel. Place the comb near the paper barrel. What happens?

The Science

Stroking the comb gave it a net negative charge. As it was brought near the neutral-charged paper barrel, it induced a charge in the paper. Negative charges on the closer side of the paper were repelled, leaving a net positive region. This region was attracted to the comb. When inertia and friction were overcome, the paper rolled toward the comb.

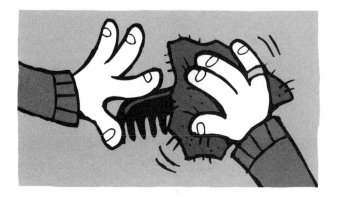

1.10 Crackles and Pops

"What's on TV tonight?"

"Arm hairs and paper scraps."

Materials

❑ a television set or computer monitor
❑ a sheet of paper

To Do

Switch the television set on. Roll up your shirt sleeve. Place your forearm against the television screen. Hear anything? Feel anything? Slowly move your arm across the screen. What happens now?

Tear up a sheet of paper into small fingernail-sized pieces. Place these pieces against the television screen and take your hand away. Do the pieces fall to the floor? Slowly move your hand just above these pieces of paper. Do any of the pieces react? If so, how? Touch several of them. Does this change their behavior?

The Science

The television screen is a charged surface. As your arm moved along the screen, it entered the screen's electric field. This field induced a charge on your arm hairs so that they became attracted to the screen. As a result, you felt them standing on end! As the hairs approached the screen, the static charge produced a small jump of electricity that made a crackling sound.

Like your arm hairs, the pieces of paper became charged by the screen's electric field. The paper's charge caused it to stick to the screen. When your hand moved above the paper, the charges shifted again to cause the paper to fly off the screen.

Check It Out! Why does a layer of dust always seem to form on a television screen?

1.11 Round the Bend

"**N**ever use an electric appliance while you are in the bathtub!"

Although it is not a great conductor of electricity, water can easily conduct the current that flows from your home's power outlet. The results are often deadly.

What about static electricity? Can water interact with non-moving charges?

Materials

- ❏ a plastic comb
- ❏ a pencil
- ❏ a plastic pen
- ❏ a piece of wool
- ❏ a sink

To Do

Turn on a water faucet. Adjust the flow to a slow but steady stream.

Pass the plastic comb through your hair several times. Slowly bring the comb close to the water. What happens?

Stroke a plastic pen with a piece of wool. Now move the pen toward the water. What happens?

Repeat this activity using a pencil. Does the pencil produce the same effect as the pen? Why?

The Science

Plastic is a good material for storing electric charges. As the comb traveled through your hair, it picked up a negative charge. When it was brought close to the running water, it induced a positive charge in the closest part of the flow. The positive water and the negative comb attracted and produced a bend in the flow. The plastic pen did the same.

As you might have guessed, wood is a poor storage material for an electric charge. The pencil did not keep enough charge to affect the water stream.

Check It Out! Could you produce a bend in a flow of water by using plastic that had been rubbed with silk?

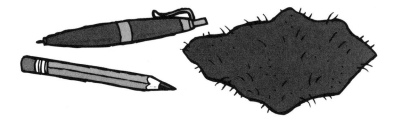

1.12 Commanding Performance

"**C**ome here."

"Walk this way."

"I command you to turn in a circle."

Have you ever wished for the power of a magic wand, a tool you can use to command the movement of all sorts of objects? Well, in this activity, you'll have a chance to build one. The "magic," however, is hidden in the invisible field of electric charges.

Materials

❑ a table

❑ a table tennis ball

❑ a plastic pen

❑ wool

To Do

Set the table tennis ball steady on a flat surface so that it sits still.

Stroke the plastic pen with the wool. After stroking the pen, move it close to the table tennis ball. What happens?

Try moving the pen so that the ball moves with a continuous motion. Can you do it?

The Science

As you stroked the pen with the wool, negative charges transferred between the materials. These charges left the wool and accumulated on the pen, giving the pen a negative charge.

When the negative pen was placed near the table tennis ball, its electric field affected the charge of the ball. The nearby negative charges were repelled by the pen and moved away. This gave one side of the ball a relatively positive charge. This positive side and the negative pen attracted. Once inertia and friction were overcome, the ball began moving.

1.13 It's a Wrap

Have you ever tried to cover a bowl with plastic wrap, only to find that the wrap seemed to have a mind of its own? You stuck one end down, and the other seemed to fly up in the opposite direction. To further complicate things, the wrap also seemed to have an uncanny attraction for both your hands. Despite having been a frustrating experience, it can be used to teach real science.

Materials
❏   lightweight plastic food wrap
❏   a wooden ruler or wooden paint stirrer

To Do
Cut a section of plastic wrap about 20 inches (50 cm) long x 2 inches (5 cm) wide. Spread this strip out flat against a wall. Rub the wrap, pressing it out in all directions.

Once it clings to the wall, peel back the wrap and hang it over a ruler. While holding the ruler with one hand, slip your other hand into the space between the sides of hanging plastic. What happens? Can you explain your observations?

The Science
As you spread the plastic wrap against the wall, charges were transferred. The plastic took on a net negative charge. The strips hanging near your hand induced a positive charge in your skin's surface. This positive charge was sufficient to attract the negative plastic wrap, which automatically drew toward your hand.

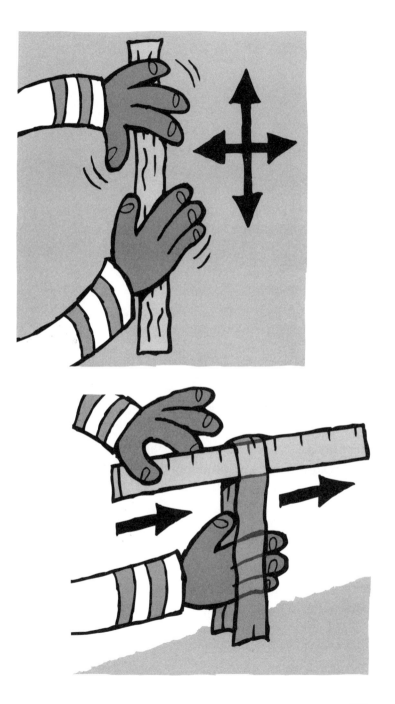

1.14 Stand Up and Be Counted

Electrical charges flow easily through metal, yet we haven't used metal in any of the experiments. Why not? Because the problem with metal is that—unlike materials such as plastic, paper, and nylon—metal is not lightweight. It's heavy, and this can easily "mask" the attraction of electrostatic forces. But for those of you who still want to experiment with metal, try this activity.

Materials

- ❑ a sheet of light-gauge aluminum foil
- ❑ a pair of scissors
- ❑ a clear plastic food container with cover
- ❑ wool

To Do

Use your scissors to cut out several human-like figures from a sheet of light-gauge aluminum foil. The figures from head to toe should be slightly shorter than the height of the plastic container (from bottom to cover).

Place the figures in the bowl. Cover the container. Stroke the container's cover vigorously. What happens?

The Science

As you stoked the plastic cover, it acquired a negative charge. This charge induced a positive charge in the near ends of the aluminum figures.

Since the heads were the lighter ends of the cutouts, they were probably the first part that moved upward. Since the charge wasn't great enough to overcome all of the figures' weight, they did not fly up and cling to the cover. Instead, the aluminum cutouts remained suspended in the air midway between the top and bottom of the bowl.

1.15 The Humidity Connection

Sometimes, static electricity experiments work great. Other times, they seem to fizzle out. Here's an experiment that will help you explore how our surroundings affect static charge.

Materials

❑   a balloon
❑   a bathroom

To Do

Find a bathroom with a shower or bathtub. Make sure that no one has bathed in the room for several hours. The room's air should be dry.

Inflate a balloon. Charge the balloon by rubbing it on your hair. What charge does the balloon acquire? Place it against the wall. Observe how it clings to the surface.

Turn on the water in the shower or bathtub. Let the room fill with humid air. Now try charging the balloon again. Place it against the wall. What happens this time?

The Science

Electric charges cannot flow well through dry air. As the balloon was rubbed against the hair, charges moved onto the balloon. However, the dry air insulated the balloon and prevented the charges from "leaking" into the surrounding air.

Electric charges flow much better in humid air. When the air was humid, charges leaked from the balloon. Since the balloon lost its charge buildup, the clinging effect (if any) was not very great.

Check It Out! Do static electricity experiments work better in winter or summer? Can you figure out why?

1.16 Doorknob Zap!

uch!

Materials

❑ a wool rug
❑ a metal doorknob

To Do

Find a room that has a rug and a metal doorknob. Turn off all the lights in the room and pull down the window shades. Put on your shoes and walk across the rug to the door.

Slowly bring your index finger toward the doorknob. What did you hear? What did you feel? What did you see?

The Science

As your shoes rub against the rug, negative charges leave it and enter your body. Although you don't feel it, your body takes on a net negative charge.

In nature, things like to be stable. Electric charges will move to create a stable, balanced condition.

As your hand nears the doorknob, negative charges concentrate at your fingertips. Just before you touch the knob, the charges have enough energy to "jump" across the gap. This jump produces a tiny spark. The spark heats the air and produces a "snap." You may feel the energy transfer as a shock.

Check It Out! Before an aircraft is fueled, a "grounding" wire must be connected to the plane's body. Why?

1.17 Clothing Zaps

Have you ever tried to separate clothes there were just taken out of a dryer? If so, you most likely encountered static cling. As the clothes were tossed in the dryer, the materials rubbed against each other and transferred charges. Clothes that became oppositely charged stuck together.

Materials
- ❑ a silk shirt
- ❑ a wool sweater
- ❑ a mirror

To Do
Put on a silk shirt. Pull on a wool sweater over the shirt.

Find a room that has a mirror. Turn off all the lights and pull down the window shades. The darker the room, the better the effect.

Stand a few feet in front of the mirror. Slowly roll up your sweater. What do you observe?

The Science
As the wool sweater rubbed against the silk shirt, charges were transferred. The shirt became negative in charge. The sweater lost electrons and became positive. The negative shirt and positive sweater attracted each other.

As you lifted the sweater, the charged materials separated. As they were pulled apart, visible sparks jumped the tiny gaps. These sparks produced a crackling sound.

Check It Out! Find out what other material combinations produce sparks. Do some combinations work better than silk and wool?

1.18 Designer Rip-Offs

Sometimes tape is a pain to work with, especially if the weather is dry and the strips are long and lightweight. They seem to attract each other. And once they make contact, their adhesive surfaces make the problem even stickier. But is this attraction real or imagined? Let's find out!

Materials

- ❑ adhesive tape
- ❑ cotton flannel shirt
- ❑ flat kitchen counter
- ❑ a pair of scissors

To Do

Cut off two strips of adhesive tape, each about 10 inches (25 cm) long. Press the strips against a flannel shirt lying flat on the counter. Keep one end of the strip free. After a moment, steadily pull both strips from the shirt. Bring the strips near each other. What happens? Can you explain why?

Repeat the activity, but this time press the strips against the kitchen countertop. Does the behavior of the strips change?

The Science

While stuck to the flannel, the tape strips gained negative charges. As the tape was pulled from the shirt's surface, these charges remained on the tape. Since both strips of tape acquired the same net charge, they repelled each other.

Check It Out! How could you use a strip of charged nylon to determine if the tape takes on a positive or negative charge?

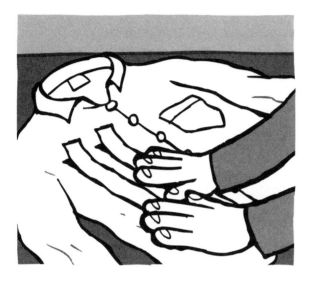

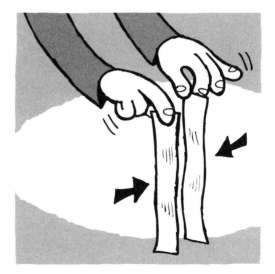

1.19 Radio Zaps

S...O...S. As the *Titanic* sank, its radio officer sent out this Morse code distress call. Each click of the telegraph's key temporarily closed an electric circuit. This circuit produced a spark, creating an invisible energy wave that traveled out from the sinking ship. These consecutive waves were detected by the antennae of other ships, carrying them by wire to a receiver. There, the invisible waves were changed into audible clicks.

Here's an experiment that illustrates how sparks were used to send Morse code messages. All you'll need is a carpet, a doorknob, and a wireless receiver (known nowadays as a radio).

Materials
- ❑ a carpet
- ❑ a metal doorknob
- ❑ a radio

To Do
Switch on a radio. Tune the radio to a frequency where no signal is detected. With the volume turned up, the radio should broadcast a low level of static.

Walk across a wool carpet wearing a pair of shoes. Approach a doorknob. While listening to the radio, reach out and touch the knob. What do you hear on the radio?

The Science
Sparks create a form of energy called an electromagnetic wave. This wave travels out through space. The antenna of

a radio can detect this form of energy. The signals it captures are carried along wires to the radio's circuitry. There, the signals are turned into sound, which is amplified and broadcast through the radio's speakers.

Check It Out! Design an experiment that shows if sparks are detected by television sets.

1.20 Static Separator

The burning of fossil fuel produces air pollution. To prevent the release of soot, some smokestacks have anti-pollution devices called *electrostatic precipitators*. These devices place a static charge on the rising soot. As the soot continues to rise in the stack, it passes through oppositely charged plates. The plates attract the soot and remove it from the smokestack gases.

Materials

- ❏ a plastic comb
- ❏ sugar
- ❏ pepper
- ❏ a small plate

To Do

Place two pinches of sugar and pepper side by side. Charge a comb by running it through your hair or stroking it with wool. Hold the comb several inches above the sugar and pepper. Slowly bring the comb closer to the mixture. Stop the comb when particles begin to jump onto it. Does sugar or pepper jump onto the comb first? Bring the comb closer to the mixture. Which particles jump onto the comb now?

The Science

Both pepper and sugar are attracted to the negatively charged comb. However, because the pepper particles are lighter, they jump first onto the comb. As the comb is brought closer to the mixture, the force of attraction increases. Eventually, this force overcomes the greater weight of the sugar grains. Like the pepper, the sugar now jumps onto the comb.

Check It Out! Can a mixture of sugar and salt be separated by static charges?

1.21 Static Jumpers

Puffed cereal grains are great materials for science experiments. Since they are light in weight, they do not require much force to move. In addition, the puffs easily transfer electric charges. Want to see? Just try this next experiment.

Materials

- ❏ puffed cereal grains
- ❏ a balloon
- ❏ a piece of wool or fur

To Do

Stuff about a dozen grains of puffed cereal into a balloon. Inflate the balloon.

Rub the balloon with a piece of wool or fur. If fabric isn't available, you can rub the balloon against your hair.

Hold the balloon by its knot, allowing it to hang. Observe the grains within the balloon. Are they stationary or moving? Touch the balloon with the fingertips of your other hand. How do the grains behave? If nothing happens, recharge the balloon by giving it twice as many strokes. Then touch it again.

The Science

As the balloon rubbed against the wool, it became negatively charged. Its negative field induced a positive charge in the nearby side of the puffed grains. This positive region was attracted to the balloon, causing the grains to cling to the balloon's negative skin.

When you touched the balloon with your fingertips, things changed. The balloon's negative charges drained out through your fingers. This created a positive region in the balloon. The charges in the grains could not shift fast enough. Instead, the positive grain surface and the positive balloon skin repelled each other. The grains jumped away.

Check It Out! Suppose a wooden rod touched the charged balloon. How might this affect the behavior of the puffed cereal grains?

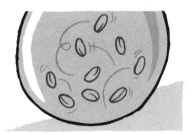

1.22 Attractive Plastic

Up and down and up and down and up and . . .

Materials

- ❑ a small section of Lucite
- ❑ two thick books (or stacks of smaller ones)
- ❑ puffed cereal or pieces of plastic foam

Hint

If your hardware or lumber store doesn't carry Lucite, check out your stationery store. The clear plastic clipboards are often manufactured from Lucite.

To Do

Place two thick books about 8 inches (20 cm) apart on a tabletop. The top of the books should be at a height of several inches above the table.

Scatter puffed cereal grains or pieces of plastic foam in the gap between the books. Place a piece of Lucite across the gap so that it rests firmly on the books.

Rub a piece of wool or felt across the surface of the Lucite. What happens to the grains below? If you observed some movement, try rubbing your hand back and forth across the Lucite. To prevent the plastic section from slipping, you'll need to steady the Lucite with your other hand. Do the grains still move?

The Science

As you stroked the plastic, it became charged through contact. This plastic's negative field affected the charge balance in the cereal grains. The grains' nearby negative charges migrated toward the farther side of the grain. This created a positive surface on each grain that was attracted to the plastic. This attraction caused the grains to jump upward and cling to the Lucite.

While the grains were attached to the Lucite, the balance changed. Electrons in the plastic moved onto the grains. Although it took them several moments to transfer, this flow eventually canceled the grains' positive charge. Without this opposite charge, the grains were no longer attracted to the plastic. They dropped off because of their weight.

Check It Out! In the 1800s, a parlor game used this principle to toss dice. Can you build this game without seeing it?

Hint

Construct the dice from plastic foam.

1.23 Gravity-Defying Peanut

As the magician chanted the magic words, the rope responded. Slowly, it appeared above the basket's rim. Up went the rope. Higher and higher it climbed, until its entire length stretched before the audience.

Materials

- ❑ a plastic foam peanut
- ❑ 1-foot-long (30 cm) thread
- ❑ adhesive tape
- ❑ a piece of wool or fur
- ❑ a balloon

To Do

Cut off a segment of thread about a foot (30 cm) in length. Tie one end of the thread to the peanut. Tape the other end of the thread to the edge of a table with the peanut hanging down.

Rub the balloon with the wool or fur, or against your hair. When the balloon is charged, slowly bring it closer to the peanut.

The peanut will be attracted to the balloon. As it moves closer to the balloon, slowly raise the balloon. Make sure that the peanut and balloon don't touch or an unwanted transfer of charges may occur. Continue raising the balloon until the peanut and thread extend perfectly upright. Keep raising the balloon. How far can you raise it and still attract the peanut?

The Science

The peanut starts out with its charge distributed evenly over its length. The negatively charged balloon induces a positive region in the peanut. This positive region and the negative balloon attract.

Since the peanut and thread are relatively light, the force of attraction can produce an interesting effect: The peanut and thread overcome gravity and rise up off the table.

Check It Out! Why would the thickness of the thread affect the ease at which the peanut can be raised?

A versorium is a device used to detect a static charge. It was invented about 400 years ago by William Gilbert, who named it from a Latin word meaning "turn around."

Materials

- ❑ a metal paper clip
- ❑ paper
- ❑ a plastic comb or pen
- ❑ a piece of wool or felt
- ❑ a pair of scissors

Hint

Doing the experiment in a transparent cup will prevent breezes from upsetting the versorium's delicate balance.

To Do

Open a paper clip into an L-shape. Unbend the larger half into a straightened length of wire. Position the smaller part as a base, so that the straightened end points upward.

Draw the pattern shown below on a sheet of paper and use a pair of scissors to cut it out.

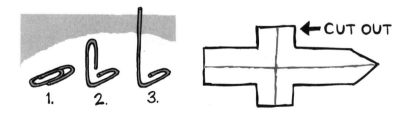

Make a slight downward crease along the dotted lines. Where they meet is the center of balance. Gently balance this pointer on the tip of the paper clip.

Charge up a plastic comb or pen with a piece of wool or felt. Bring the pen close to the versorium. What do you observe? Can you get the pointer to turn an entire circle?

The Science

The charged object induced a positive region in the folded paper. This positive region and the negative comb attracted each other. The force was great enough to spin the pointer in any direction.

Check It Out! Can the needle of a versorium be made of aluminum foil?

1.25 On the Edge

Although gravity can be a mighty force, it requires huge masses for its effects to be readily observed. Not so with electricity. In fact, a minor charge can easily be observed using a tool that is often associated with measuring an object's length.

Materials

❑   a wooden ruler
❑   a balloon

To Do

Position the ruler so that it balances on the edge of a table. At this balance point, the ruler remains steady with one end lifted slightly from the tabletop.

Charge up the balloon by stroking it on your hair or with a piece of wool. Slowly approach the raised end of the ruler with the charged balloon. What happens? How does the electrostatic force work against the force of gravity?

The Science

When the ruler was balanced, it remained still. As the charged balloon was brought near one end of the ruler, it upset the wood's balance of charges. The negatively-charged balloon induced a positive charge in the near end of the ruler. This positive charge and the negative balloon attracted each other. The force of attraction was great enough to offset the balance of mass and cause the end of the ruler to rise.

1.26 Repelling Peanuts

As you've learned, like charges repel while unlike charges attract. You've also observed how charges can be transferred from one object to another. The following experiment uses both these concepts. After building it, figure out how this tool might be used to measure charges.

Materials

- ❑ a metal clothes hanger
- ❑ 12-inch-long (30 cm) thread
- ❑ two plastic foam peanuts
- ❑ a balloon

To Do

Hold the hanger's hook with one hand. Firmly grasp the long side of the hanger with the other. Slowly and steadily pull out the hanger until it looks like a stretched-out diamond.

Bend up the lower half of the diamond to form a stand. Give the hook a quarter turn so that it falls back toward the center of the stand.

Tie a foam peanut to each end of a 12-inch (30 cm) thread. Drape the thread over the upturned hook of the hanger. Position the thread so that the peanuts hang at the same level.

Inflate a balloon. Charge the balloon by rubbing it with a piece of wool or fur. Bring the balloon near the peanuts. How do the peanuts react? Touch the charged balloon to the peanuts. What happens now?

The Science

The lightweight peanuts were easily influenced by electric charges. When the balloon was brought nearby, it caused the charges within the peanuts to separate. The regions of the peanuts nearest the balloon became positive and were attracted to the negative balloon.

When the charged balloon touched the peanuts, electrons flowed. This electron flow caused both peanuts to become negatively charged. Since they had the same charges, the peanuts repelled each other with enough force for them to separate and rise. The distance that they separated depended on the strength of the charge they acquired. This distance can be used as a method for measuring the strength of electrical charges.

Check It Out! Suppose the peanuts were placed on separate hanger supports. Would this affect their behavior?

1.27 Light the Light

Did you know that fluorescent lightbulbs are called "cool lights?" They get this name from the cool temperature at which they operate. Unlike regular filament bulbs, fluorescent lights don't need to heat up in order to produce light. The light given off by a fluorescent bulb comes from a special chemical that coats the glass. When this chemical is struck by charges, it lights up. Cool!

Materials

- ❑ a fluorescent lightbulb
- ❑ an incandescent (filament) lightbulb
- ❑ a piece of wool
- ❑ a balloon

To Do

Go into a dark room. Gently stroke the filament bulb with the wool. Observe its outer coating. Can you detect any light?

Now stroke the fluorescent bulb. After several minutes, examine its outer coating. What do you see? How does stroking each bulb affect the production of light?

Rub a balloon on your hair. Hold this charged balloon near the fluorescent bulb. What happens when a spark jumps between the bulb and the balloon?

The Science

An incandescent bulb needs to get "white hot" in order to produce light. In contrast, a fluorescent bulb doesn't depend upon heat in order to generate light. When the bulb was stroked by the wool, its surface became charged. As some of the charges jumped about, they excited the light-producing chemicals in the bulb's coating. These "energized" chemicals produced the faint glow on the bulb's surface. Likewise, when the spark jumped from the balloon to the bulb, it produced a visible flash.

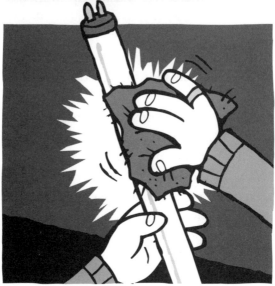

1.28 Flying Leaves

In the laboratory, scientists measure static charge with an electroscope, a tool that shows the relative strength of a charge. Here's an inexpensive electroscope that you can build at home.

Materials

❑ a clear plastic cup
❑ aluminum foil
❑ a metal paper clip
❑ modeling clay
❑ a balloon
❑ a pair of scissors

Hint

The stout tumbler-type plastic cups work best.

To Do

Have an adult drill a small hole in the center of the cup's bottom. The hole must be wider than the wire of a paper clip.

Cut two small strips of aluminum foil about ¼ inch (6 mm) x 1½ inches (3.75 cm). Use an unbent paper clip to punch a tiny hole near one end of each strip. Press and flatten the foil. These foil pieces are the "leaves."

Open a paper clip and bend it to form a long "j." Hang the leaves on the bottom part of the "j." Insert the shaft of the paper clip into the underside of the cup. Make sure that the leaves clear the rim of the cup. Use a small lump of clay to secure the clip in place.

Roll a piece of aluminum foil into a small ball. Secure the ball to the end of the paper clip.

Charge a balloon by rubbing it with a piece of wool or fur. Slowly bring the balloon toward the cup. What happens to the leaves of the electroscope? Pull the balloon away. How do the leaves react?

The Science

As you brought the balloon near the electroscope, it induced a charge. The balloon's negative charge repelled the electrons in the ball of aluminum foil. These electrons traveled down the clip into the leaves. Both leaves acquired a negative charge. Since like charges repel, the leaves flew apart.

Check It Out! Design and construct a similar electroscope that uses a material other than aluminum foil.

1.29 Bubble Charge

Soap bubbles represent a delicate balance of forces. Water tension creates the force that holds the thin film of the bubble together. Soap within the bubble solution offsets this force and allows the bulbbles to stabilize. This results in a lightweight sphere whose shape is easily changed by static forces, as you will see.

Materials

- ❑ bubble solution
- ❑ a drinking straw
- ❑ a mug or plastic container
- ❑ a balloon

To Do

Fill a mug one-third full with bubble solution. Insert a straw into the solution. Blow into the solution with a slow and steady exhale. A mountain of bubbles should climb over the rim of the mug.

Charge a balloon by rubbing it against your hair. Move the balloon close to the bubbles. What happens? Describe how the bubbles become distorted. Is the attraction strong enough to "rip" a bubble from the mug?

The Science

Like plastic foam peanuts and puffed cereal grains, soap bubbles react strongly to static charges. Their light weight and ease of charging make them ideal subjects for studying the effects of static attraction.

As the charged balloon approached the bubbles, negatively charged particles nearby migrated to the far side of the bubbles. This created a bubble surface with a positive charge, which was attracted to the negative balloon. This attraction caused the bubbles to stretch out and form an egg shape.

Check It Out! Will a bubble blown from a wand also react to a charged balloon? Make a guess and then find out.

PART TWO

Current Electricity

Warning! The activities in the following section should be done only with 1.5-volt flashlight cells. Do not use any other batteries, current sources, or electric outlets!

2.1 Coming to Terms

Do you get tired of reading instructions? Everyone does. Wouldn't it be great for the only instruction to be "Have fun!" Well, this is it. There are no specific instructions for this activity. All you have to do is mess around with the following materials. Who knows? You might light a bulb and, in the process, discover a whole bunch of things about electricity.

Materials

- ❑ one "D" cell battery
- ❑ a length of electrical wire with 1½ inches (3.75 cm) at each end stripped bare of insulation
- ❑ one flashlight bulb

To Do

Have fun!*

*If you're looking for a challenge, try lighting this bulb.

The Science

Since the idea here is just to have fun, the science can wait. For now, understanding some basic terms will be helpful.

Is it a battery or a cell?

It depends on who you are. Most people, who aren't scientists or science teachers, call them batteries.

"The flashlight needs more batteries."

"The camera died. It needs a new set of batteries."

People in science, however, tend to call these energy devices cells. The size (and electric force) of a cell is identified by letters. For example, the large cell that fits in a flashlight is a "D" cell. The smaller cells that power iPod™ are "AA" cells.

Scientists use the term *battery* for a number of cells hooked together.

Is it a bulb or a lamp?

Again, it depends upon how scientific you want to sound. While most people call it a bulb, scientists call it a lamp, which indicates a thing that emits light. To scientists, a bulb can be anything from a flower part to a squishy rubber contraption.

What's meant by a cell's polarity?

All cells have a positive (+) pole and a negative (-) pole. In a household cell, the end with the raised cap is the positive pole, or positive terminal. The flat end of the cell is the negative pole, or negative terminal. Electrons are pushed out of the cell at the negative pole and return to the cell at the positive pole after traveling through the external circuit.

2.2 Battery Holder

Think about the fun you had in the previous experiment. You probably wished that you had a few extra hands to hold down wires and keep things connected. If you don't have a lab assistant or a little sister or brother handy, you might free up your hands by constructing some laboratory devices.

This first one is a battery (okay, *cell*) holder.

Materials

❑ a thick rubber band that fits snugly over a battery
❑ two brass paper fasteners
❑ two 1-foot-long (30 cm) electrical wires with 1½ inches (3.75 cm) at each end stripped bare of insulation

To Do

To make this battery holder, push a brass paper fastener through the middle of a thick rubber band. Bend back the "legs" so that the fastener remains anchored in the band as shown.

Insert a second fastener likewise into the opposite side of the rubber band. Again, spread the legs back to secure the fastener.

Turn the rubber band inside out so that the caps of the fasteners face inward (the legs should be on the outer surface). Slip the rubber band over a cell. Attach one wire to each of the fasteners. Remember that the ends of the wire must be stripped of insulation in order to make electrical contact.

To test the holder, touch the free ends of the connecting wires to a flashlight bulb (okay, *lamp*).

The Science

If the holder doesn't work, make sure that the legs of the clips and the connecting wires have an electric contact. The end of the wire should be free of any insulation. If you are using a bell wire (a thick wire that science teachers always seem to have), make sure to strip the plastic covering from the ends, of the wire. If you are using enamel-painted wire, you'll need to scrape off the painted surface with sandpaper or emery cloth. Then, make sure that the caps of the fasteners are positioned against the terminals of the cell.

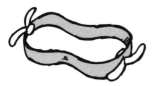

2.3 Bulb Holder

Now that your hands are free, you can build one more device: a bulb holder.

Materials

- ❑ a metal paper clip
- ❑ masking tape
- ❑ two connecting wires with 1½ inches (3.75 cm) at each end stripped bare of insulation
- ❑ a flashlight bulb
- ❑ one "D" cell battery

To Do

While holding the paper clip's outer loop, gently bend the inner loop downward so it looks like this:

Wrap masking tape across the gap in the smaller loop. This wrapping should form a "ledge."

Wind the bare end of a wire around the wrapping. Make sure that the tape insulates the clip from the wire (see below).

WRAPPING OF TAPE ➤   ADDED WIRE ➤

Wrap the bare end of a second wire around the middle bent region of the paper clip.

Insert a flashlight bulb into the larger loop. The threads of the bulb should fit snugly against the clip. As you turn the bulb, it should "screw" into the holder. The bottom terminal of the bulb should press firmly against the exposed wire wrap. You may have to bend the clip in order to adjust the contacts.

Once you have constructed the holder, test it by connecting the contact wires to a "D" cell. Don't worry if the light does not glow brightly. As long as it lights, your lamp holder is fine.

The Science

If your lamp didn't glow as brightly as you might have hoped, here's why: All lamps are designed for a specific voltage. Often this value is stamped on the bulb's metal collar. Most flashlight bulbs need 3 volts to shine their brightest. At lower voltages they emit less light. A single "D" cell has only 1.5 volts and, therefore, can't energize this lamp to its brightest state.

Check It Out! You can, however, buy bulbs designed to shine most brightly at 1.5 volts.

Note
Never connect a bulb to more voltage than it is designed to handle. The extra voltage will produce a flow of current that can burn out the filament (thin thread inside the bulb) and destroy the bulb!

24 Switch

Take a look around you. If you're indoors, there's most likely a wall switch nearby.

Behind the wall, the switch is connected to electrical wires that lead to a light fixture. When you flip the switch to the "on" position, the light goes on. Flip the switch "off" and the light magically goes off. What's happening back there to make the light go on and off?

Materials

❑ a small block of wood
❑ two thumbtacks
❑ a metal paper clip
❑ two electrical wires with 1½ inches (3.75 cm) at each end stripped bare of insulation

To Do

Position two thumbtacks several inches apart on a small block of wood. Push them partially into the wood, leaving only a small space between the head of the tack and the wood surface.

Wrap a bare end of one of the electrical wires around one of the thumbtacks. Push this tack into the wood to secure the wire.

Unbend a paper clip to make an S shape. Slip one end of the S under the second thumbtack. Wrap this same thumbtack with the bare end of the second wire. Push the tack into the wood to secure both the wire and the paper clip.

Make sure the paper clip can reach over the first thumbtack. If not, work its shape a little more. When you press down on the paper clip, it should make contact with the head of the first thumbtack. When you release it, the clip should spring up and "open" the circuit.

The Science

The flow of electricity requires an uninterrupted path through which an electric charge can move. The charge will stop flowing if there are any breaks in the path. It doesn't matter where the break is. As long as the path is broken, no current will flow.

A switch is a device that *opens* and *closes* a circuit. In the "on" position, the switch closes the circuit and completes the route for flowing current. In the "off" position, the switch places a gap in the path, which halts the current's flow.

2.5 Drawing a Circuit

How well do you draw? Do your lightbulbs look like lightbulbs or do they resemble the heads of aliens from outer space?

Although this next experiment involves drawing, don't worry. You don't have to be an artist. All you have to do is copy simple symbols and arrange them to represent electric circuits. So pick up your pencil and give it a try!

Materials

❑   a pencil
❑   a sheet of paper

To Do

Examine the symbols on the opposite page. They represent different parts of a circuit. Can you figure out what the complete circuit looks like? Look at the next page to find out.

Now it's your turn. Use these symbols to draw diagrams that represent the following circuits. Don't forget about the cells' polarity and to illustrate it correctly.

The Science

Symbols and diagrams are helpful. Find help with this one at the bottom of page 81.

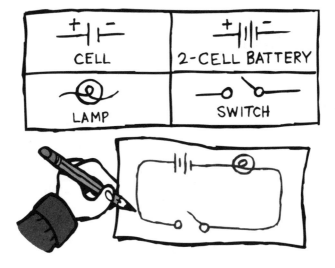

+ −		+ −
—⊣├—		—⊣║├—
CELL		2-CELL BATTERY
—◯⟋—		—○ ⟋○—
LAMP		SWITCH

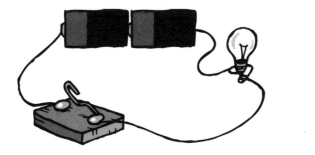

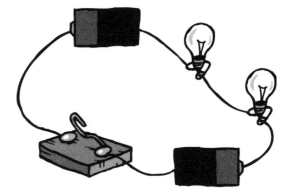

2.6 Conductivity Tester

Slice a bell wire in half and you'll find a copper core surrounded by a plastic covering. The inner copper strand provides the path for electron flow. The outer covering is a very poor conductor of electricity. It cloaks the copper to prevent electricity from traveling out of the wire and into other conductors (such as *you*—zap!).

Materials

- ❑ a "D" cell in a battery holder
- ❑ a flashlight bulb in a lamp holder
- ❑ electrical wires with 1½ inches (3.75 cm) at each end stripped bare of insulation
- ❑ a variety of materials, such as coins, aluminum foil, compact disks, keys, costume jewelry, rings, and spoons

To Do

Assemble the circuit shown on the next page to make a conductivity tester. It can show you how well a material conducts electricity.

Touch the bare ends of the two wires together and the lamp should light. If not, check your connections. Place the material to be tested on the tabletop. Touch the wires to opposite sides of the material, making sure the wires don't touch each other. Does the lamp light? If so, what do you know about the material's ability to offer a path for electron travel? Suppose the lamp doesn't light. What then?

The Science

Some materials, such as metals, are formed by atoms that have a *loose* hold on their electrons. Since the electrons are not tightly bound to individual atoms, they can be passed easily among neighboring atoms. The "passing" of electrons forms a movement of charge known as an electric current. Materials that permit easy electron flow are called *conductors*.

Other materials, such as glass and plastic, are formed by atoms that have a *tight* hold on their electrons. These atoms resist passing electrons from neighbor to neighbor. This resistance produces a material that acts as an *insulator*.

Dimmers are cool devices. These circuit components are often attached to ceiling lights or floor lamps. As you rotate the dimmer knob, the light gets brighter or dimmer.

Materials

- ❏ a pencil (or just a piece of pencil lead, which is really graphite)
- ❏ two "D" cells in battery holders
- ❏ one flashlight bulb in lamp holder
- ❏ electrical wires with 1½ inches (3.75 cm) at each end stripped bare of insulation

To Do

Have an adult use a wood-carving tool to shave down one side of a pencil so that 2 inches (5 cm) or so of graphite is exposed. It should look like this:

If you don't have an adult to do the carving, do *not* do it yourself! Instead, find a piece of graphite made for use in refillable pencils.

Assemble the circuit below.

Touch the bare ends of the two wires together and the lamp should light. If not, check your connections. Now place the ends of both tester wires against the graphite. What happens? Slowly move these wires farther apart long the length of graphite. What happens to the brightness of the lamp? Can you explain your observations? Predict what will happen if the wires are moved closer together. Find out if your prediction is correct.

The Science

Unlike copper, graphite isn't a good conductor of electricity. When electricity flows through graphite, it crashes head-on into resistance. This resistance cuts down the flow of electricity.

When your circuit included only a small section of graphite, the lamp remained bright. As the wires were drawn apart, the current was forced to travel a greater distance through the graphite. This extra distance produced increased resistance, which cut down the electrical current and made the bulb dimmer.

Answer to Experiment 2.5

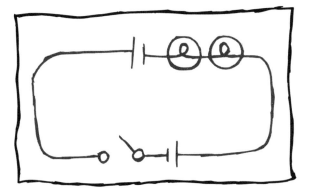

2.8 Short Circuit

Pop Quiz

Question: What would happen if the positive and negative terminals of a cell were connected by a wire without placing a bulb, motor, or some sort of resistance in the circuit?

Answer: If the circuit were left on for more than a few minutes, you'd destroy the cell and, if the current source was strong enough, you'd burn yourself or start a fire.

Materials

❑ two "D" cells in battery holders
❑ one flashlight bulb in lamp holder
❑ two switches
❑ electrical wires with 1½ inches (3.75 cm) at each end stripped bare of insulation

To Do

Assemble the circuit below.

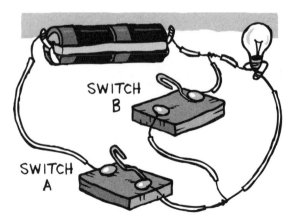

SWITCH
B

SWITCH
A

Close only switch A. What happens to the lamp? Is there a closed circuit? If so, trace the complete circuit through which electricity flows.

Close only switch B. What happens to the lamp? Is there a closed circuit? If so, trace the complete circuit through which electricity flows.

Bend the clip in switch A so that this switch remains on. While the lamp is glowing, close switch B. What happens? What path does the current follow when both switches are closed? Why? Release switch B. What happens now? Why?

The Science

Switch A controls current flow in the outer loop. When switch A is closed, current flows along this outer path to light the lamp.

Switch B is part of a separate path that offers no resistance. When switch B was closed, its path became complete. Since the path contained no resistors, it acted as a short circuit. The electrons always take the path of least resistance. The current flowed across switch B and bypassed the lamp. Without a current flow, the lamp went out.

Check It Out! Short circuits can cause fires. When a wire offers little or no resistance to current flow, excessive flow can heat up the conductor. If the wire gets hot enough, it can cause burns and start fires.

2.9 A Limited Path

Have you ever tested old batteries in a 2-cell flashlight? If so, you know that both the cells need to be working. If one cell has leaked, the flashlight won't work. No matter how strong the other cell is, if one cell is bad, the light won't go on. That's because the electricity needed to light the bulb must flow through both cells. If one cell is dead, the path is blocked. There's no way around it.

Materials

❑ two "D" cells in battery holders
❑ two flashlight bulbs in lamp holders
❑ a switch
❑ electrical wires with 1½ inches (3.75 cm) at each end stripped bare of insulation

To Do

Assemble the circuit shown below.

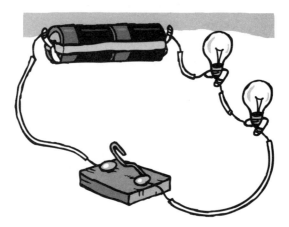

Close the switch. What happens? Do both bulbs light? Is one bulb brighter than the other? In this circuit, how many different paths can the electrons flow through?

Keep the switch closed. Unscrew one of the bulbs. What happens? Can you explain your observations?

Draw a diagram of this circuit using the symbols presented earlier. Use this diagram to describe the flow of electrons.

The Science

The circuit you built is called a *series circuit*. It offers only one path for the moving charges. All the electrons must travel through the same circuit components.

If one of the wires is broken (or one of the components removed), the circuit is opened. All current stops! That's why the other bulb went out, even though it remained attached to the circuit.

2.10 A Path with More Options

At the holidays and at parties, you often see strings of hanging lights. They decorate homes and stores everywhere. Years ago, when one bulb failed, the whole string always went out. These days when one bulb goes out, the string stays lit most of the time.

That's because some of these light sets are connected up in a special way. When one bulb goes out, the others remain lit! This special way of wiring makes it much easier to identify the burned-out bulb. Otherwise, you'd be faced with testing the entire set like in the old days.

Materials

- ❏ two "D" cells in battery holders
- ❏ two flashlight bulbs in lamp holders
- ❏ electrical wires with 1½ inches (3.75 cm) each end stripped bare of insulation
- ❏ a switch

To Do

Assemble the circuit shown below.

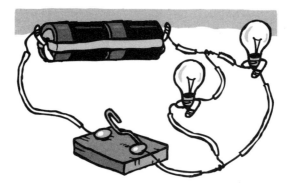

Close the switch. What happens? Do both bulbs light? Is one bulb brighter than the other? In this circuit, how many different paths can the electrons flow through?

Keep the switch closed. Unscrew one of the bulbs. What happens? Can you explain your observations?

Draw a diagram of this circuit using the symbols presented earlier. Use this diagram to describe the flow of electrons.

The Science

The circuit you built is called a *parallel circuit*. It offers more than one path for the moving charges. This circuit had two possible paths. The current of flowing electrons split up. Half the current traveled through the nearer "arm" of the circuit. The other half traveled through the distant "arm."

This time, when a bulb was removed, the remaining bulb stayed lit. That's because the path to the untouched bulb remained intact. The electrons continued to flow along the completed circuit loop.

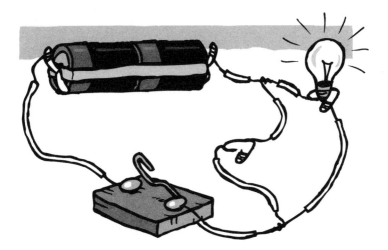

2.11 The Basic Buzzer

In the next activity, you'll assemble a simple circuit that contains a buzzer. This working circuit will be used in several of the following experiments. First, you need to find the components, make sure they match up, and assemble the circuit correctly.

Materials

❑ a 1.5-volt or 3-volt buzzer or bicycle horn
❑ one or two "D" cell batteries
❑ battery holders
❑ electrical wires with 1½ inches (3.75 cm) at each end stripped bare of insulation
❑ wire stripper

Caution

Do not use any buzzer that requires more than two "D" cell batteries.

To Do

Find a buzzer or bicycle horn. Buzzers can sometimes be found on old board games. If you do remove the buzzer from a game, write down the type and number of cells needed to energize it. Remember, you'll need to match your battery supply to the electrical needs of this device.

If you don't find a board game buzzer, a bicycle horn might work. Some horns can be removed from their streamlined case. If so, you'll need to identify the terminals to the horn. If the horn can't be separated from the case, remove the cell. Attach wires to the terminals that are exposed inside the battery holder. These wires can then be attached to your circuit as direct paths to the horn. Again, you'll need to match up the horn with the correct power supply.

If you can't scavenge the parts, there's always the local electronics or home improvement store. They should have both 1.5-volt and 3-volt buzzers.

Your simple circuit should look like that shown on the opposite page. In the following experiments, you'll add this circuit to different types of switches. Before you do, make sure that the buzzer works.

The Science

When the circuit is complete, electricity flows. This current of electrical charges "energizes" the horn or buzzer, causing its sound-producing parts to vibrate. We detect the vibrations as a *bzzzzz*.

2.12 Secret Switch

Alarm systems are pretty cool, especially the high-tech ones that detect intruders by the heat they give off. In this experiment, you'll get to construct an alarm device and use it within a circuit.

Materials

- ❏ 2 electrical connecting wires with 1½ inches (3.75 cm) at each end stripped bare of insulation
- ❏ a piece of simple buzzer circuit (see p. 88)
- ❏ 10 inch x 3 inch (25 cm x 7.5 cm) cardboard
- ❏ a pair of scissors
- ❏ 2-inch-long (5 cm) strip of aluminum foil
- ❏ adhesive tape

To Do

Cut a strip of cardboard (removed from a packing box) about 10 inches (25 cm) long x 3 inches (7.5 cm) wide. Fold the strip in half to form two 5-inch-long (12.5 cm) sections. Wrap the middle of each section with a 2-inch-long (5 cm) strip of aluminum foil. Use tape to secure the foil. Attach two 1-foot-long (30 cm) wires to the outer side of each foil strip. Attach these wires to a series circuit that contains two 1.5-volt cells and a buzzer. Place the folded cardboard beneath a carpet or mat. Make sure that the weight of the carpet doesn't press the halves together. Once the alarm detector is "set," just sit back and wait.

The Science

This alarm device is a pressure switch. The weight of the carpet is not great enough to fully press the cardboard halves together fully. Therefore, the circuit remains open. When someone stands on the carpet, however, their added weight closes the circuit. Once closed, the current will flow from the battery to the buzzer and sounds the alarm.

2.13 Door Alarm

Have you ever seen a cartoon in which someone removes a tooth by using a string tied to a doorknob? As the door slams shut, the string tugs at the loose tooth and yanks it out. Ouch! In this experiment, you'll do something a little less alarming by opening a door.

Materials
❑ electrical wires with 1½ inches (3.75 cm) at each end stripped bare of insulation
❑ a simple buzzer circuit (see p. 88)
❑ a piece of cardboard
❑ a pair of scissors
❑ a metal paper clip
❑ adhesive tape
❑ two metal thumbtacks
❑ string
❑ a small square piece of paper

To Do
Cut a strip of cardboard (removed from a packing box) about 5 inches (12.5 cm) long x 3 inches (7.5 cm) wide. Push two metal thumbtacks into the cardboard. The tacks should be about 2 inches (5 cm) apart. Wrap a length of electrical wire around the shaft of each tack.

Unbend a paper clip into an S shape. Slip one end of the S around the base of one tack. Adjust the bend in the paper clip to ensure that there is enough pressure to keep the far end of the clip pressed down on the second tack.

Slip a small square of paper between the paper clip and the tack. The paper should be held in place by the pressure of the bent clip.

Tape one end of a piece of string to the paper and tie the other end to a doorknob. Attach the electrical wires to a series circuit that contains two 1.5-volt cells and a 3-volt buzzer.

Tape the cardboard setup near the door so that it remains secure. Now invite a friend to open the door. *Bzzzzzzzzzzzzz.*

The Science

The paper between the clip and the tack acted as an insulator. This insulator blocked the flow of electric current. When the paper was yanked away, the clip and tack made contact. When the circuit was thus completed, charges flowed and the alarm sounded.

2.14 Steady Hands

Have you ever played the electrified board game in which you operate on a patient? If your hand isn't steady, the forceps strikes the conducting metal. Instantly a loud sound confirms that you "grounded out" and lost your turn. In this experiment, you'll have the chance to build another type of game that also tests your steadiness.

Materials

- ❑ a metal coat hanger
- ❑ a simple buzzer circuit (see p. 88)
- ❑ two lumps electrical wires with 1½ inches (3.75 cm) at each end stripped bare of insulation
- ❑ steel wool

To Do

Use steel wool to remove any sort of coating or lacquer that covers the coat hanger. Make sure that you remove this coating outdoors and don't breathe in any of the material.

Untwist the coat hanger and bend it into a large U. Make several bumps in the middle section of the U. Stand the hanger up by setting its ends into lumps of clay.

Assemble the battery of two D cells. Attach an electrical wire from one base of the clothes hanger to one terminal of the buzzer. Attach another electrical wire from the other terminal of the buzzer to one of the ends of the battery. Now attach the 2-foot-long (60 cm) electrical wire to the other end of the battery. Bend the free end of the 2-foot-long (60 cm) wire into a small loop that fits around the coat hanger.

The object of this game is to move the wire loop along the entire path and not make contact with the hanger.

The Science

In order to win, you have to maintain an open circuit. If your hand is not steady, the loop will make contact with the conductive hanger. Once contact is made, the circuit becomes complete and the buzzer sounds to announce your defeat!

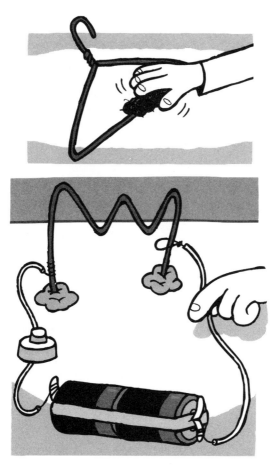

2.15 The Magnetic Connection

Electricity-carrying cables are often buried underground. To pinpoint their exact location, utility workers use a tool that detects magnetic fields. Within the cables, the current of flowing charges produces a magnetic field that extends into the surrounding space. By detecting this magnetic field, workers can locate the exact position of the unseen electric flow.

Materials

❑ two "D" cells in battery holders
❑ electrical wires with 1½ (3.75 cm) inches at each end stripped bare of insulation
❑ a switch
❑ an index card
❑ iron filings
❑ a compass

To Do

Assemble the complete circuit shown below. Place an index card on top of a section of wire so that you can't see it.

Turn the switch to the "on" position for a few minutes only. Otherwise, you will damage the cell. Lightly sprinkle iron filings onto the card. Tap the card gently. Do the filings form a pattern or do they scatter randomly? Can you explain your observations?

Turn the switch to the "off" position. Carefully return the iron filings to their container.

Place a compass alongside the wire. Note the direction in which the needle points. While watching the needle, turn the switch to the "on" position. What do you observe? Explain what you see.

Suppose you switched the connectors to the cells so that their polarity was reversed. How would that affect the direction in which the needle points? Make a guess and then find out by switching the connections. Was your guess correct?

The Science

Electric currents produce a detectable magnetic field. The filings that fell onto the index card felt the force of the magnetic field. Their final position formed a pattern that followed the magnetic lines of force that extended outward from the wire.

Likewise, the compass needle also felt the magnetic force. When the current flowed, it produced a magnetic attraction that successfully competed with the Earth's magnetic field.

2.16 Upstairs/Downstairs Switch

"**D**id you hear that? It sounds like a saliva-dribbling alien monster banging around at the bottom of the stairs—or maybe it's just a dog."

"Should I turn on the light?"

"Sure. But I'm not going down there."

"No need to. There's a light switch right here at the top of the stairs."

Materials

❑ two "D" cells in battery holders

❑ 1 flashlight bulb in lamp holder

❑ six thumbtacks

❑ 2 metal paper clips

❑ 2 pieces of wood or thick foam core

❑ electrical wires with 1½ (3.75 cm) inches at each end stripped bare of insulation

To Do

For this activity, you'll need to build two new switches. The switch bases are made from two small blocks of wood. Carefully push three thumbtacks partially into the wood base as shown on the opposite page. Unbend a paper clip and wrap it around the thumbtack that is on the side by itself. Don't push the tacks fully into the wood until the wire connections are in place.

Now assemble the circuit below using these two switches. Unlike the previous switches, these circuit parts are sliding switches. The paper clip is constantly pushed against the top of one tack or the other. When you slide the paper clip from one tack to another, you complete or break a circuit. This circuit remains "on" until you slide the clip off the tack.

Flip one switch. What happens? Flip the other switch. What happens now? Which switch controls the lamp? Explain.

The Science

The circuit is constructed so that both switches are on the path over which the electric current flows. Flipping either switch changes the circuit. If it's open, a flipped switch will close the circuit. If it's closed, a flipped switch will open the circuit. As you might infer, this type of switch is useful when you want to control a light from more than one location.

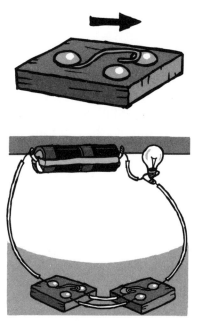

2.17 Meet a Meter

An electrician has a special tool to measure the current that flows through wiring. The tool is called a multimeter and it is capable of measuring several properties of electric flow. In this experiment, you'll build a simple type of meter that also responds to the flow of current.

Materials

- ❑ 3 yards (3 m) of 24-gauge insulated copper wire
- ❑ wire strippers
- ❑ packaging tape
- ❑ a sewing needle
- ❑ thread
- ❑ a strong bar magnet
- ❑ a juice can
- ❑ 1 "D"-cell battery

To Do

Strip several inches of insulation from both ends of the wire. Wrap this wire around the can into a tight coil, leaving about 1 foot (30 cm) of wire at each end of the coil. Slip the coil off the can. Wrap several pieces of packaging tape around the coil to secure its shape. Use a larger piece of tape to stick the coil onto a flat surface so that it stands up.

Stroke the needle against the magnet at least forty times in the same direction to magnetize it.

Tie a small length of thread around the middle of the needle so that it hangs level. Tape the other end of the thread to the top of the wire coil. The magnetized needle should balance in the middle of the coil's open space.

Touch the free ends of the wires to the positive and negative sides of the "D" cell battery. What happens? Switch the wires to touch the opposite sides of the cell. What happens now?

The Science

When the wires were attached to the cell, electricity flowed through the coil. This movement of charge created a magnetic field. The magnetic field affected the magnetized needle, causing it to spin and change its pointing direction. When the wires were switched, the current flowed in the opposite direction. In response, the needle turned and pointed in the opposite direction.

2.18 Lemon Cell

Have you ever heard of a potato clock? If so, you may believe that this device uses two potatoes to generate the energy to power a clock. Right? Wrong. The potatoes don't generate the electrical flow. The potatoes are merely solid structures though which charges can flow. The parts that produce the flow of charges are the two different metals that are stuck into the potato. Want to learn more? Read on.

Materials

❑   a lemon
❑   a copper penny
❑   a strip of zinc (obtained from hardware store)
❑   steel wool
❑   a knife
❑   a current meter (assembled in "Meet a Meter," p. 100)

To Do

Use the steel wool to polish the surfaces of the penny and the zinc strip. File down any sharp edges on the zinc strip.

Have an adult use the knife to punch two small slits into the lemon's tough skin. The slits should be about ½ inch (12.5 mm) in length and placed about ¼ inch (6 mm) apart.

Insert the penny into one of the slits. Insert the zinc strip into the other slit. Make sure that the metals don't touch.

Touch the leads of the current meter to the exposed metals. What happens to the magnetized needle? Can you explain your observation?

The Science

There is a natural tendency for electric charges to travel between different metals (in this case, copper and zinc). Within the lemon, the acid environment offered a partial route for the travel of charges. The route was completed by the external circuit, which included the coiled wire. As the current traveled through this coil, it produced a magnetic field. This field deflected the needle from is original pointing direction.

Check It Out! Can other pairs of metals produce a detectable current? Try replacing the zinc with an old silver coin or a wad of aluminum foil.

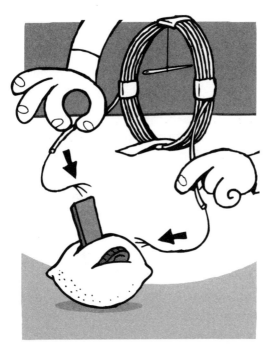

2.19 Battery of Cells

A single cell made of two metals can produce only a
small "push" of charge. To increase this push,
several cells can be wired together. This arrangement of
side-by-side cells forms an electrical device known to
scientists as a *battery*.

Materials

- ❑ 3 pennies
- ❑ 3 iron washers
- ❑ steel wool
- ❑ blotter paper
- ❑ a pair of scissors
- ❑ salt
- ❑ water
- ❑ a current meter (assembled in "Meet a Meter"
  experiment, p. 100)

To Do

Polish the coins and washers with steel wool. Use a pair of
scissors to cut the blotter paper into four penny-sized
circles.

Soak the paper in salt water. Sandwich a damp paper
circle between a penny and a washer. Test the generation
of electricity with your current meter by touching one lead
of the meter to the coin, the other to the washer. How does
the meter react?

Stack up the other metal pieces, alternating pennies
and washers, to make two other sandwiches. Pile the three
sandwiches so that there is a circle of saltwater-soaked

blotter paper separating each sandwich. No two pieces of metal should make direct contact.

Use tape to secure this three-cell stack. Retest the current. Is it stronger? Can you explain your observations?

The Science

The simple penny/washer cell produced a very small amount of electricity. As the cells were joined together, they formed a battery. The three-cell battery generated three times the electricity of a single cell. This increase produced a more noticeable deflection of the meter's needle.

Check It Out! A car battery is made of six side-by-side but separate cells. These cells are wired together to produce six times the energy available from only a single cell.

2.20 Generating a Connection

So far, the electricity you've generated has been produced by chemical reactions. Although this source of electricity is important, most of your electricity at home is produced by generators. Generators are large devices that convert the energy of spinning magnetic fields into electric current.

Materials

- ❑ a strong bar magnet
- ❑ 3 yards (3 m) of 24-gauge insulated copper wire
- ❑ a juice can
- ❑ adhesive tape
- ❑ a current meter (assembled in "Meet a Meter," p. 100)

To Do

Strip several inches of insulation from both ends of the wire. Wrap this wire around the can into a tight coil. Leave about 1 foot (30 cm) of wire at each end of the coil. Slip the coil off the can and secure its shape with several pieces of tape. Attach the bare ends of these wires to the ends of the current meter's wires to form a complete circuit containing two coils.

Push the bar magnet in and out of the newly assembled coil. What happens to the needle that is suspended in the current meter? Can you explain your observations?

The Science

Congratulations! You've just generated electricity. As the
magnet moved in and out of the coil, it induced a back-
and-forth flow of charges within the coil. This flow moved
throughout the circuit. At the meter, this alternating
current produced a flip-flopping magnetic field. Its effects
were seen by the needle, which continually changed
directions.

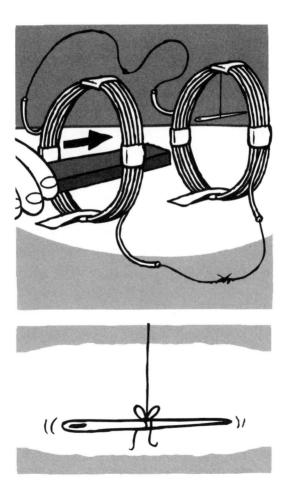

2.21 Magnetic Coil

Use your bar magnet today. Put it away. If you take it out tomorrow, most likely it will still be a magnet. Take it out the next day and you'll find that it still has magnetic properties. That's why it's called a *permanent magnet*. But permanent doesn't mean forever. Over time, the magnet will lose its magnetic strength.

Materials

- ❑ electrical wires with 1½ (3.75 cm) inches at each end stripped bare of insulation
- ❑ a pencil
- ❑ a nail
- ❑ 2 "D" cells in battery holders
- ❑ a switch

To Do

Wrap a length of bell wire around a pencil so that it forms a tight coil. Make sure to leave plenty of wire free at each end so that the coil can be attached to a circuit.

Once the coil is made, slip it off the pencil and use it to construct the circuit on the next page.

Close the switch. Touch the coil to some small paper clips or thumbtacks. What happens? Can the coil lift these items? Release the switch. What happens now?

Slip an iron nail into the coil (as shown on the opposite page). Tighten the coil around the nail by pulling on the wire ends. Now close the switch and try to pick up some clips or thumbtacks. What happens? How has the presence of an iron core affected the magnetic strength of this coil?

Important

Turn this circuit on for *only* a few minutes at a time. Then turn it off. Otherwise, the cells will be ruined.

The Science

The flowing current creates a magnetic field. The field can be increased by wrapping the straight wire into a coil. It can be boosted even further by inserting an iron core into the center of the coil.

Check It Out! Some junkyards use giant electromagnets. At the flick of a switch, these awesome magnets can pick up or drop huge automobiles and vans.

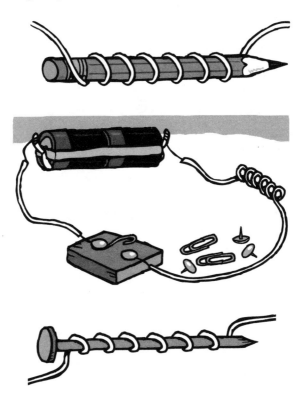

2.22 Morse Code Transmitters

For your last electrical experiment, you'll construct a Morse code station, or telegraph.

Materials

- ❑ 4 "D" cells in battery holders
- ❑ 2 flashlight bulbs in lamp holders
- ❑ 2 switches
- ❑ 4 brass fasteners
- ❑ plenty of electrical wire with ends stripped bare of insulation

To Do

Assemble two separate Morse code stations that look like this one at right:

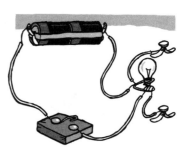

Next, place the two stations at different locations and connect them by wire. Begin by setting them up side by side. This will make solving any connection problems much easier and quicker.

Use two lengths of connecting wire to attach the stations as shown at right.

If this short connection works, you're ready to expand. Use more connecting wire and place the stations at opposite ends of your room. Do the transmitters still work? If so, you're ready.

Have an adult help you set up a pair of wires that will connect two stations placed in different rooms of the house.

Important

Make sure that connecting wires aren't placed where they will get in the way and accidentally trip someone.

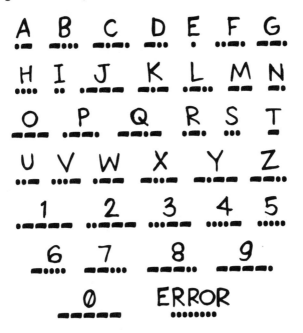

The Morse Code

Make two photocopies of the Morse code chart above. Keep a copy by each station.

Below each letter and number is the code that represents it. The circles are "dots." A dot is transmitted by a quick on/off press of the switch. The small rectangles are "dashes." A dash is transmitted by a longer on/off press.

This code was developed by a man named Samuel Morse. In 1838, Morse invested the first device that could send coded messages along electric wires. The system used for relaying message came to be called *Morse code.*

The Science

When either switch (called a key on a telegraph) is closed, the double-lamp circuit becomes complete. The current flows from the closer pair of cells through the large connecting loop of wire (strung between the stations). Flowing along this wire, the electricity lights both lamps. By monitoring your own bulb, you can make sure that your message has been sent to the other station. When you see a light, your friend will see a light.

PART THREE

Magnetic Attraction

3.1 Field Trip

Close your eyes and think of a refrigerator door. What comes to mind? For most of us, it's of all sorts of paper—math tests, photographs, and grocery lists— hanging on the door by an assortment of magnets.

Although magnets and refrigerator doors seem inseparable, magnets can also stick to many other objects and materials. To begin your first adventure in the field of magnetism, start in the kitchen. Everything you need for this experiment can be found there.

Materials

- ❑ a refrigerator magnet
- ❑ paper
- ❑ a pencil

To Do

Remove a magnet from the refrigerator door. Pick one that is large and strong. Use this magnet to test which of the following kitchen materials and objects it attracts. Make sure to record your findings on a sheet of paper.

- ❑ refrigerator door handle
- ❑ other refrigerator magnets
- ❑ sink basin
- ❑ water faucet
- ❑ plastic wrap
- ❑ wad of crumpled aluminum foil
- ❑ spoon
- ❑ cooking pot
- ❑ frying pan

- ❑ copper water pipe
- ❑ food cans
- ❑ doorknob
- ❑ cabinet latches

The Science

As you've discovered, the magnet doesn't attract all the tested items. An object's attraction to a magnet depends upon the composition of its material. You'll learn more about what is and isn't attracted to magnets as you try the fun and interesting activities that follow.

Have you ever seen a science fiction show about an invisible monster or alien? If so, what trick did the hero finally use to "see" the monster? Was the monster splattered with paint? Was it coated with water? Perhaps its outline could be shown by the way its force field distorted the surrounding air.

Although magnetic fields may not be as dangerous as invisible aliens, they can be just as interesting. The only problem is that you can't see them ... or can you?

Materials

- ❑ paper
- ❑ iron filings
- ❑ a bar magnet

To Do

Position a bar magnet under a sheet of paper. Make sure that the paper remains level.

Lightly sprinkle iron filings over the paper. Tap the paper. Observe the pattern that the filings make as they fall onto the surface. Does the pattern contain straight or curved lines? Do these lines completely encircle the magnet? If not, where do the lines of force meet the magnet?

The Science

All magnets are surrounded by an invisible field patterned by the magnet's lines of force. Although the lines, the force, and the field are invisible, we can reveal their patterns with a light dusting of magnetic material.

Iron filings are light, small, and readily attracted to magnets. The filings on the paper formed a pattern mirroring the lines of force in the magnetic field.

Check It Out! Guess what magnetic pattern a horseshoe magnet will produce. Then check it out with a magnet and filings.

Have you ever bought a foul-tasting cereal just to get the prize that was buried at the bottom of the box? If you're like most kids, you have.

If you were lucky enough to discover a compass, you're all prepared for this next activity—providing you still have the compass, and it works. A compass has more than a navigational use. It's also a handy tool for mapping out invisible magnetic fields.

Materials

- ❑ a bar magnet
- ❑ a compass
- ❑ paper
- ❑ a pencil

To Do

Place a bar magnet in the center of a sheet of paper and carefully trace its shape.

Now place the compass on the same sheet of paper a few inches from the magnet. Trace its outline on the paper. Observe the direction in which the compass needle points. Pick up the compass from the paper and draw the direction in which the needle was pointing. Place the compass in another spot nearby. Again, trace its outline and draw in the direction of the needle. Repeat this step until a pattern emerges.

The Science

A compass needle is a tiny, lightweight magnet. It reacts to both Earth's magnetic field and to the fields of any nearby magnets. When it was placed close to the bar magnet, the needle rotated so that it aligned with the invisible field of the magnet. By moving the compass, you were able to reveal the extent and direction of the bar magnet's lines of force.

In the first experiment, you discovered that not all metals are attracted to magnets. Some, such as the refrigerator door handle, had strong magnetic properties. Others, such as wads of crumpled aluminum foil, lacked this attraction.

So what's the story with metal? Why are some metals attracted to magnets while others have no reaction?

Materials

❑   a strong kitchen magnet
❑   an assortment of metal items, such as a metal paper clip, steel nail, brass screw, stripped copper wire, stainless steel utensil, penny, nickel, dime, quarter, and any other materials whose magnetic properties you want to test.

To Do

Test the above objects to find out whether they have magnetic properties. Steadily bring a magnet near the test object. Does the object move? Is the attraction strong enough to lift the object? What force must be overcome if the magnet is to lift the object off a surface?

The Science

All materials are made up of tiny building blocks called atoms. Every atom has its own magnetic field, which is produced by its moving electrons. In most materials, the tiny atomic fields point in completely random directions. Because of their randomness, these tiny fields cancel each other out: one pulls right, another pulls left; one pulls down, another pulls up, etc.

The magnetic fields of a few materials, such as iron and nickel, can be made to all point in the same direction. So instead of canceling out each other's force, the forces line up and make the material magnetic.

Check It Out! The composition of U.S. coins has changed over the years. Have any coins ever been magnetic? In what years?

Suppose the smallest of all particles acts like a tiny, free-spinning magnet. Now imagine a material composed of a vast landscape of these side-by-side force fields. If all of the individual magnetic fields pointed in different directions, they'd cancel each other out. Some would pull in one direction, others would pull in another. However, if all of the fields pointed in the same direction, the individual forces would pull together and produce what we observe as magnetism.

Materials

❏   iron nails
❏   a bar magnet
❏   a magnetic compass

To Do

Hold a magnet several inches from a magnetic compass. Move the magnet and observe any movement of the compass needle. What happens to the compass needle as the magnet moves?

Hold an iron nail several inches from the compass. Move the nail and observe any movement of the compass needle. What happens to the needle as the nail moves?

Now hold the nail in one hand and the bar magnet in the other. Stroke the magnet along the length of the nail. All strokes must be applied in the same direction and with the same end of the magnet. After several dozen strokes, retest the nail's magnetism. Does it make the compass needle move now?

The Science

The iron nail is made of a material that can be magnetized. Before being stroked by a magnet, the nail's atoms have magnetic fields that point in all directions, which cancel each other out.

As the nail is stroked, the magnetic fields of its atoms are influenced by the field of the bar magnet. The atoms "feel" the magnetic pull and begin to "point" in a common direction. Eventually enough fields "pull together" to produce detectable magnetic properties.

Check It Out! Design an experiment that tests how back-and-forth strokes induce magnetism.

3.6 Unmaking a Magnet

Do you think you can strip a nail of its magnetic properties? If so, how?

Hint

When the magnetic fields of atoms align, magnetism is produced. Therefore, if you were able to break up the atomic pattern, you'd destroy the magnetic properties.

Materials

- ❏ 1 magnetized nail
- ❏ a hammer
- ❏ a magnetic compass
- ❏ safety goggles
- ❏ shop bench vise

Caution

Perform this activity only under adult supervision. Wear safety goggles when striking the nail.

To Do

First use the magnetic compass to test the magnetic properties of the magnetized nail. Observe how far the attraction between the nail and the compass needle extends.

Place the nail on a shop bench vise. Put on a pair of safety goggles. Use the hammer to gently tap the nail several times. Retest the nail's magnetism. Is the nail still magnetic? Has it lost any of its magnetic force?

The Science

Magnetism depends upon the direction of each atom's magnetic poles (or opposite ends). When the poles of many atoms align, the whole object takes on magnetic properties. By striking the nail with the hammer, you produce tiny changes in the position of its atoms. Although the changes are small, they are enough to affect the strength of the magnetic field. Since fewer atoms' magnetic fields point in the same direction, the nail loses some of its magnetic force.

Check It Out! Design an experiment that examines the effects of low temperatures on magnets.

3.7 Shake It Up, Baby!

The previous experiment proved that hammering definitely shakes things up! It pushes some atoms this way, others that way. The atomic jumble ruins the magnetic pattern by producing random magnetic directions that cancel each other out.

But you don't need a hammer to shake things up. A simple back-and-forth shake gets the same results.

Materials

- ❏ iron filings
- ❏ a compass
- ❏ a magnet
- ❏ a small plastic vial

To Do

Fill a small vial with iron filings. Gently circle the vial with a compass. Does the compass needle react to the filings?

Hold the vial still. Stroke a strong magnet down the side of the vial in one direction. (Remember: back-and-forth movements will undo the magnetic fields that they produce.)

After several dozen strokes, circle the vial once more with the compass. Does the needle now react to the filings? Can you guess what happened?

Put a cap on the vial and shake up the filings. Once more, try the compass test. What happens now? Can you explain what you see (or don't see)?

The Science

At first, the filings were not magnetized. However, after the magnet stroked the vial, the filings took on magnetic properties. The filings' field was strong enough to be detected by the compass. When the vial's contents were shaken, the individual filings moved about. At an atomic level, their tiny magnetic fields were no longer aligned. This field hodgepodge canceled itself out and, as a result, the filings lost their magnetic properties.

3.8 Polar Journey

Have you ever met someone who is your complete opposite? You're sloppy and they're neat. You're loud and they're quiet. You're into science, they *hate it*. Opposites, ugh!

But what about magnets? Are they also repelled by opposites, or is there something more, something almost *attractive* about being different?

Materials

- ❑ 1-foot-long (30 cm) piece of thread
- ❑ two clothes pins
- ❑ plastic foam packing peanuts
- ❑ a bar magnet

To Do

Stroke the magnet along the length of one pin. All strokes must be applied in the same direction (from the head end to the point end) and with the same pole of the magnet. After several dozen strokes, the pin should be magnetized. Magnetize a second pin in the same manner.

Insert one of the magnetized pins into a foam peanut. Gently tie a 1-foot–long (30 cm) piece of thread around the peanut so that the pin hangs level. Tape the free end of the thread to the edge of a desk. The pin/foam should hang freely.

Bring the head of the second magnetized pin close to the head of the hanging pin. What happens? Try bringing the points of both pins together. What happens now? Now try bringing a head and a point together.

The Science

Each pin has two poles—a north pole and a south pole. Since both pins were magnetized in the same way, their heads were magnetized with the same pole. Likewise, each point took on the same magnetic pole. When the pin heads were brought together, they repelled because like charges repel one another. Likewise, the two points on the pins also repelled. In contrast, when the point and the head were brought together, they attracted each other because unlike (or opposite) poles attract.

Check It Out! Using a compass, can you identify the pole at the head and the point of the pin?

3.9　Poles Versus Middle

"I say it's the poles."

"Well, I say it's the middle."

"Poles."

"Middle."

"*Poles!!*"

"*Middle!!*"

Why not perform a test that will show which (if either) part of the magnet is stronger? That's what a scientist would do.

Materials

- ❑ a bar magnet
- ❑ a bunch of metal paper clips

To Do

Hold the bar magnet by one of its ends. Bring the other end of the magnet (a pole) into contact with one paper clip. Lift the clip into the air.

Slip together the loops of two paper clips to form a chain. Try lifting the chain with the opposite end of the magnet. Keep increasing the number of paper clips in the chain until you've reached the longest chain that can be picked up by the magnet's pole.

Make a prediction. Will the other pole of the magnet pick up more, fewer, or the same number of paper clips? Explain your thinking.

Now touch the center of the magnet (between the poles) to a paper clip. Try lifting the clip into the air.

What happens? How does the magnetic strength at the center of the magnet compare with the magnetic strength at the poles?

The Science

As you've just discovered, the poles of the magnet have the stronger force. If you were to "see" the magnetic force field, you'd find the lines of force converging—coming together—at the poles. This balanced pattern illustrates the equal strength of the north and south poles. There are far fewer lines of magnetic force near the magnet's middle. This results in a smaller magnetic attraction. Paper clips that are placed here will either drop from the magnet or slide over to the stronger pole regions.

Think about It. Why does the shape of a magnetized horseshoe result in its greater lifting capacity?

3.10 Chain Game

Every horror movie buff knows that when a person is bitten by a vampire, he or she will soon transform into one of the undead. Those people subsequently bitten by this new vampire will also become vampires, as part of a deadly chain. From bite to bite, victim to victim, the chain of vampires continues. Magnets have their own way of passing along certain properties.

Materials

- ❑ a bar magnet
- ❑ a dish
- ❑ a handful of small iron washers

To Do

Fill a dish with small iron washers. Gently lay the magnet across the pile. Slowly pick up the magnet. What do you see? Do the washers form a hanging bridge? What part of the magnet do they stick to? Can you explain why the washers behave as they do?

The Science

A magnetic force can travel "through" magnetic objects. The poles are the strongest regions of the magnet. The magnetic force "flows" from these poles to the washers that are in physical contact with the magnet. Those washers become magnetized and act, in turn, as magnets. Any washers in contact with these magnetized washers also become magnetized, so that the magnetic force is transmitted down the line to any washers in contact with a magnetized washer. Finally, the magnetized links from both ends of the magnet meet up and form a hanging chain.

Two thousand years ago, Chinese navigators figured out how magnets could be used in navigation. Some people believe this connection was discovered when someone dropped a piece of natural magnetic rock (called lodestone) into a bucket of water. The rock settled so that it "pointed" to the north. Every time it was dropped, the rock came to rest pointing in the same direction.

Materials

- ❑ a sewing needle
- ❑ a magnet
- ❑ a plastic foam cup
- ❑ a pair of scissors
- ❑ a bowl half filled with water

To Do

Carefully remove the circular bottom of a plastic foam cup and place this separated piece on the surface of the water. Observe how it floats.

Stroke the magnet down the length of the needle. Remember to stroke in only one direction. Place the magnetized needle on the floating foam cup bottom. What happens to the needle and cup bottom?

Place the magnet along the side of the bowl. Move the magnet around the bowl. Now what happens to the needle?

The Science

Earth has a magnetic field. Magnetic objects within this field will react to this attractive force. When the magnetized needle was placed on the floating foam cup bottom, it spun freely. Under the influence of Earth's magnetic field, the needle on its raft rotated to its most stable position. Eventually, it came to rest with its north-seeking end pointed to the magnetic North Pole.

Check It Out! A compass on a large ocean vessel is usually located between two spheres. Do some research on the Internet or in some books to find out what these spheres do.

3.12 Patterns of Attraction

Water has a skinlike covering formed by the way water molecules attract each other. This attraction is called *surface tension*. Lightweight objects such as needles and pins float effortlessly on this invisible "skin." Needles and pins are also easily magnetized. These facts can combine to make an interesting experiment.

Materials

- ❑ a dozen sewing needles or pins
- ❑ a magnet
- ❑ a non-metal bowl
- ❑ water
- ❑ a metal paper clip

To Do

Magnetize about a dozen needles by stroking a permanent magnet along their length. Remember to stroke in only one direction.

Fill a bowl three-fourths-full with water. Unbend a paper clip to form a right angle between its end loops. Use this paper clip as a "cradle" to lower needles onto the water's surface.

Place several needles on the water's surface. Observe how their ends react to each other. What causes some of the needles to attract and others to repel?

Take a look at the shapes shown at the top of the opposite page. Can you steer the needles into the patterns at the top of the opposite page? Good luck.

Caution

Needles and pins have sharp points. Be careful when handling them. Make sure that when you are finished using these or any other sharp objects, all of them are accounted for (and none are left in the bowl).

The Science

Two major concepts are at work here. The first is surface tension, which is formed by attractive forces between neighboring water molecules. The second concept is magnetism. As you have learned, like poles repel, while unlike poles attract. In order for needles to align end to end, the adjoining ends must have opposite charges. Once they are positioned correctly, the magnetic force helps keep their shape.

Check It Out! Can you build a magnetic "raft" that can support the weight of an extra-large paper clip?

3.13 Floating Magnets

Can metal magnets actually resist the pull of gravity? Hard to imagine, but they can. The notion may seem like something from a science fiction movie, but it's merely another demonstration of magnetic repulsion.

Materials

❑ 4 circular magnets with holes in their centers (available at local electronics stores)
❑ a 6-inch-long (15 cm) wooden dowel, ¼-inch (6 mm) in diameter
❑ a flat wooden base
❑ carpenter's wood glue

To Do

Cut a piece of ¼-inch (6 mm) wooden dowel about 6 inches (15 cm) long. Make sure that both ends are flat and smooth. Position the dowel in the center of the flat wooden base. Secure it to the base with a bead of carpenter's wood glue. Let it dry.

Slip a magnet over the dowel. Slip another one on top. If the magnets attract, remove the upper magnet. Flip it upside down and replace it on the dowel so it is repelled by the magnet below. The upper magnet will appear to float and bounce in the air. Add several more magnets. Make sure that each magnet repels the magnets on either side of it.

The Science

As you've learned, like poles repel and unlike poles attract. You create a force of repulsion by positioning like poles next to like poles. This force is strong enough to keep the upper magnets suspended in the air.

Check It Out! Could you keep adding magnets without ever having like poles come in contact? Give it a try!

3.14 Lively Drawing

Here is an experiment that blends art and science. This combination can produce effects that are sometimes almost magical. You'll construct a drawing that has moving parts. The parts, however, aren't magical—just magnetic.

Materials

- ❑ 2 pieces of poster board or stiff cardboard
- ❑ a box of crayons
- ❑ colored markers
- ❑ adhesive tape
- ❑ a bunch of metal paper clips
- ❑ a pair of scissors
- ❑ a small magnet

To Do

Draw a colorful setting on the poster board, anything from a city street to the Grand Canyon. We show a fish tank.

On a separate piece of poster board, draw several objects that will move around within the setting, such as helicopters, cars, or tropical fish. Use a pair scissors to carefully cut out their outlines. Color the objects. Tape a paper clip on the underside of each cutout.

Brace the poster board upright. Position a movable cutout on the scene. Place a magnet behind the board so that it is opposite the object's paper clip. As you move the unseen magnet, the object will move within your scene.

What happens to the object when you stop moving the magnet? What happens to the object when you remove the magnet from the back of the board?

The Science

Magnetic fields can easily pass through paper. When the magnet was placed behind the poster board, it attracted the paper clip. The force was so strong that the clip remained held against the upright surface.

Check It Out! Create an animated story using your setting and characters. Videotape it and show it to your friends.

3.15 Iron-filled Breakfast

Iron is a nutrient that is essential for maintaining good health. It helps form a chemical within the blood called hemoglobin, which is found in red blood cells. There, it transports oxygen from the lungs to every cell in the body. Without iron, we couldn't make hemoglobin and our cells would die from lack of oxygen.

Materials
- ❏ iron-enriched cereal
- ❏ a strong magnet
- ❏ a piece of white paper
- ❏ plastic bag
- ❏ a spoon

To Do

Place a spoonful of iron-enriched cereal into a small plastic bag. Use the back end of the spoon to crush the cereal grains. Keep crushing them until all the grains are made into a fine powder.

Carefully pour the powder onto a sheet of clean, white paper. Place a strong magnet underneath the paper. Slowly move the magnet back and forth. What do you observe?

The Science

Iron-enriched cereal contains the element iron. The iron is bound up in the cereal grains. When the grains are crushed, the small fragments containing iron are released.

These fragments are lightweight enough to respond to magnetic fields. The cereal dust on the paper "dances" to the movement of the magnet below.

Check It Out! Crush a daily vitamin pill that is iron-enriched and do the same experiment. Can you observe any evidence of iron in the pill?

3.16 Magnetic Muscle

Like people, magnets come in all shapes and sizes, and these differences are easy to see. But magnetic strength is not so obvious. Is there some way to test and create a scale of relative magnetic strength? Let's test some magnets to find out.

Materials

- ❑ a bunch of metal paper clips
- ❑ a piece of 1-foot-long (30 cm) string
- ❑ a wooden or plastic ruler
- ❑ a stack of books
- ❑ a variety of magnets

To Do

Cut a length of string about 1 foot (30 cm) long. Tie one end of the string to the center of a magnet. Tape the other end to the end of a ruler. Position the ruler so that the magnet extends beyond the edge of the desk and hangs free. Secure the ruler with a small stack of books.

Place a paper clip in your palm. Raise the clip so that it touches one pole of the hanging magnet. Gently lower your hand. Is the magnet strong enough to hold onto the clip?

Slip together the loops of two paper clips to form a chain. Repeat the magnet test. Can the magnet support two clips? Next, try three. Keep going until you reach the limit that this magnet can support.

Repeat this experiment with all the magnets.

The Science

Magnets vary in strength. You can determine their relative strength by comparing how many paper clips each magnet can support.

Keep in mind that over time, magnets lose some of their power. The magnetic fields of individual atoms start "pointing" in different directions. As more atoms begin to point randomly, the magnet loses strength.

Check It Out! Do you wear an electric wristwatch? If so, you should be careful when handling powerful magnets. Some magnets can produce a magnetic field strong enough to ruin watches and other electronic devices.

3.17 Magnetic Extension

Suppose a paper clip is placed against the north pole of a strong magnet. Does the end of the paper clip in contact with the magnet also become a north pole? If so, will the entire clip be a "northern extension" of the magnet and lack any sort of south pole? Or will the whole clip become a south pole and lack any northern identity? Maybe it will have both a north and a south pole? Maybe neither? Make a guess and then explore the nature of the paper clip's poles.

Materials
- ❑ a metal paper clip
- ❑ a strong bar magnet
- ❑ a compass

To Do

Place the end of the magnet near the compass. Observe and record which end of the magnet the compass needle determines is the north. Now place a paper clip at the magnet's north end. The clip should be positioned so that it extends straight out from and parallel to the magnet.

Place the compass near the free end of the magnetized paper clip. Which end of the compass points to the free end of the clip? Can you explain what you see? Suppose the compass is brought near the contact point of the clip and the magnet. In which direction will it point?

The Science

When a paper clip is placed in contact with the magnet, magnetism is induced in the clip. The clip "lengthens" the magnet by extending the pole. The paper clip's poles will mirror those of the magnet.

Check It Out! Although magnets can have more than two poles, there are no known magnets that have only one pole. All magnets have at least one north pole and one south pole.

3.18 Flying Saucer with Cup

Do you like to confuse people? If so, this next experiment may be just the thing. It's an impossible sight that's made possible by a magnet's invisible force field.

Materials

- ❑ paper
- ❑ colored markers or crayons
- ❑ a metal paper clip
- ❑ a piece of string 10 inches (25 cm) long
- ❑ adhesive tape
- ❑ a strong flat magnet
- ❑ a stack of books
- ❑ a pair of scissors

To Do

Draw and color in a small picture of a coffee cup sitting on top of a saucer. Cut out your drawing.

Cut a length of string about 10 inches (25 cm) long. Tie one end of the string to the paper clip. Tape the paper clip to the back of the coffee cup drawing. Tape the other end of the string to a desk.

Hide a flat magnet between the pages of a book. Place this book atop a stack of other books. Position the stack so the picture is attracted to the hidden magnet. The cup and saucer should float in mid-air with no apparent reason for the gravity-defying behavior.

The Science

Although it isn't visible, the magnetic field exists. The hidden magnet's attraction is strong enough to overcome the weight of the clip, paper, tape, and string.

Check It Out! Suppose the paper clip was replaced by another magnet. How might this change the effect?

 **3.19 Field Blockers**

Now that you've had some experience with magnetic fields, it's time to make some predictions. Examine the list below and circle the materials that you believe will block a magnetic field.

- ❏ aluminum foil
- ❏ wood
- ❏ a piece of videocassette tape
- ❏ an audio CD
- ❏ a plastic plate
- ❏ coins

Now test your predictions by doing the following experiment.

Materials
- ❏ a metal paper clip
- ❏ a piece of string 10 inches (25 cm) long
- ❏ adhesive tape
- ❏ a strong magnet
- ❏ a wooden or plastic ruler
- ❏ a stack of books
- ❏ the materials listed above

To Do
Cut a length of string about 10 inches (25 cm) long. Tie one end of the string to the paper clip. Tape the other end of the string to a desk.

Tape a magnet to the end of a ruler. Insert the ruler between the pages of a book so that the magnet extends out as far from the book as possible. Place this book on top of a stack of several books.

Position the stack so that the magnet is directly above the paper clip. The clip's string should be short enough to allow a gap between the clip and the magnet, but long enough for the clip to remain supported by the magnet's attraction.

Insert various objects between the magnet and the clip. Record how the magnetic field behaves.

The Science

Some materials (those made of iron) will block a magnetic field. Most materials, however, will not and will allow the magnetic field to penetrate.

Check It Out! Can you magnetize a length of videotape that has been removed from a discarded cassette?

3.20 Auto-Motion

Here's another one of those just-for-fun experiments.

Materials

- ❏ foam core board
- ❏ colored markers
- ❏ a pair of chopsticks
- ❏ two magnets
- ❏ stiff paper
- ❏ a bunch of metal paper clips
- ❏ adhesive tape
- ❏ four books of the same width

To Do

Sketch a bird's-eye view of a roadway on a large piece of foam core board. The road should split, connect, and form several intersections. Include things like houses, factories, rivers, and garages along the road. Elevate the board by supporting each corner with a book.

Copy the car shown below onto a piece of stiff paper. You may wish to draw other vehicles, such as fire engines, ambulances, and construction trucks. Bend the paper along the dotted line. Tape a paper clip to the upper surface of the lower fold (see illustration below). Put the car on the roadway of the foam core board.

Tape a magnet to the end of a chopstick. Place the end of the stick with the magnet under the car on the foam core board. As you move the stick, the car should move along the roadway.

The Science

Form core does not interfere with magnetic fields. Magnets placed underneath the board attracted the paper clip vehicles. As the magnets moved, they dragged the paper clips (and their attached vehicles) across the foam core's surface.

Check It Out! Try building a magnetic airport or harbor.

3.21 Separation by Magnet

Okay, who did it? Who mixed the iron filings with the salt? Got any bright ideas about how to separate these two substances?

Materials
- ❑ a sealable plastic bag
- ❑ a magnet
- ❑ 1 teaspoon (5 mL) salt
- ❑ plate
- ❑ ¼ teaspoon (1.25 mL) iron filings

To Do

Add about ¼ teaspoon (1.25 mL) of iron filings to 1 teaspoon (5 mL) of salt. Mix well and pour this blend onto a plate.

Seal the magnet in the plastic bag. Predict what will happen when you move the magnet through the mixture. After you make your prediction, try it and see what happens.

The Science

The iron filings are attracted to the magnet and stick to the plastic bag's outer surface. The salt (which isn't a magnetic material) remains behind.

Another Solution

Add the salt-and-iron mixture to a large container of warm (not hot) water. Stir vigorously. The salt crystals will dissolve in the water, breaking down into invisible atomic-sized particles. These particles mix so thoroughly in water that they won't sink or accumulate at the bottom. This type of mixture is called a *solution*.

In contrast, iron won't dissolve in water. Its particles remain unchanged. The filings merely fall and accumulate at the bottom of the container.

If this solution is poured through filter paper, the dissolved salt flows through with the water. The iron filings, however, will be trapped by the paper.

Index

Answers to Check It Out!

p.9 corners of an equilateral triangle; p. 11 yes; p. 13 yes; p. 15 yes; p. 23 too heavy; p. 27 induction of charge; p. 29 yes; p. 37 winter/drier; p. 39 prevent sparks; p. 41 many including glass/silk, rubber/fur; p. 43 observe attraction/repulsion to positive nylon; p. 45 inquiry based upon ability of TV to broadcast spark cracks; p. 47 difficult—too similar in weight; p. 49 insulator materials would not ground out charge; p. 51 dice tossed by Lucite attraction; p. 53 thickness increases thread weight; p. 55 yes; p. 59 depends upon charging procedure; p. 63 replace aluminum with thin plastic; p. 65 yes; p. 103 yes, replacement produces less current; p. 117 similar-looking force lines that connect side-by-side poles; p. 123 compare and contrast magnets made with one-way to back-and-forth strokes; p. 125 measure magnetic strength of magnets placed in freezer; p. 129 analyze attraction/repulsion behavior; p. 131 two side-by-side poles pull together; p. 139 no—weight would eventually press bottom magnets together; p. 145 filter out the unwanted magnetic fields; p. 149 greater space between magnets; p. 151 yes

About the Author

 Michael Anthony DiSpezio is a renaissance educator who writes, speaks, and offers workshops in science throughout the world. He received an M.A. in biology from Boston University, while working at the time as a research assistant to a Nobel Prize winner.

After tiring of counting hairs on copepods, Michael traded the marine biology laboratory for the classroom. Over the years he has taught a varied assortment of science and mathematics courses.

To date, Michael is the author of *Super Sensational Science Fair Projects, How Bright Is Your Brain?, Space Mania, Weather Mania, Dino Mania, Map Mania, Optical Illusion Magic, Eye-Popping Optical Illusions, Critical Thinking Puzzles, Great Critical Thinking Puzzles, Visual Thinking Puzzles,* and more (all from Sterling). He is also the co-author of over thirty elementary, middle, and secondary school science textbooks. He has also developed a wide range of material for clients including the Discovery Channel, Weather Channel, Disney, Children's Television Workshop, and Scientific American Frontiers.

Michael's work has taken him from Jordan (part of the Middle East Peace Accord) to the Daytime Emmy Awards where one of his projects was nominated for "Most Outstanding Show for Children." In 2005, he hosted dozens of live television shows and presented to 20,000 students in a major sports arena.